TOKYO TRAVEL GUIDE 2024

ESSENTIAL UP-TO-DATE TIPS FOR SAFE, SMART, AND STRESS-FREE ADVENTURES - NAVIGATE BUSY STREETS AND QUIET SPOTS LIKE A PRO

KAIYO TAKUMI

Title: Tokyo Travel Guide 2024

Author: Kaiyo Takumi

Publisher: Kaiyo Takumi

Publication Date: February, 16 2024

Edition: First Edition

Contact:

tokyoguide2024@gmail.com

CONTENTS

DISCLAIMER AND READER'S NOTE

Before we join on this adventure together, there are a few important notes we'd like to share to ensure your experience with this guide is both enriching and accurate.

Travel Information Accuracy: While we have gone to great lengths to ensure that the information contained within this book is accurate as of 2024, the dynamic nature of travel means that details such as opening hours, prices, and travel advisories can change. We recommend verifying any critical information through official sources or local contacts before making travel arrangements.

Digital Experience: This print version of our travel guide contains black and white photographs that offer a glimpse into the beauty and diversity of Tokyo. For those who crave the full visual feast, the Kindle version of this guide includes all photographs in vibrant color, enhancing your planning and reading experience.

Your Feedback Matters: Your journey with this book doesn't end when you close its pages. We invite you to leave a review on the platform where you purchased this guide. Your insights and experiences are invaluable, not just to us but to fellow travelers navigating their paths based on this guide.

Handle with Care: Treat this book as your travel companion. Just as you would navigate the roads, alleys, and landscapes of Tokyo with care and curiosity, we encourage you to approach the information and insights within these pages with the same openness and respect. Our goal is to inspire, inform, and ignite your passion for exploration.

Thank you for choosing this guide as your doorway to Tokyo. Whether you're reading to plan your next adventure or to wanderlust from the comfort of your home, we're thrilled to be part of your journey.

Safe travels,
Kaiyo Takumi

INTRODUCTION

How to Dig Into This Book

Think of this guide as your personal roadmap to Tokyo. It's laid out to help you easily find what you're after, whether that's checking out the famous spots, finding the best time to visit, or uncovering some hidden gems that most tourists don't know about. Start wherever you like – jump to the sections that grab your attention first or follow it from start to finish to build up your Tokyo know-how layer by layer. Each chapter's loaded with cool places to check out, tips to make your journey smoother, and a bunch of insights to get you under the skin of this buzzing city.

What's Inside

Here's the deal: we've crammed this book with everything from the lowdown on Tokyo's crazy transport system to advice on where to grab the best eats without blowing your budget. You'll get the scoop on the city's epic sights, the low-key spots where you can escape the crowds, and even how to navigate Tokyo's customs like you've been doing it your whole life. Plus, we've thrown in loads of awesome photos and stories to get you hyped about what's waiting for you.

A Heads-Up

Just a quick note to let you know that we've used some smart tech (yep, Artificial Intelligence) alongside the author's own experiences to pull together the freshest, most accurate info for you. This means you're getting the best of both worlds – cool tech and real-deal insights from someone who knows what they're talking about.

Copyright Stuff

All the awesome images and killer content in this book? They're copyrighted, which means they're ours, and you gotta respect that. If you're not sure what's cool and what's not, check out the copyright section to get the lowdown. Don't go sharing or copying stuff without permission – no one wants to deal with that kind of drama.

Is This Book for You?

We gotta be straight with you – this book isn't for everyone. It's for the curious souls, the adventure seekers, the ones who want to dive deep and really get what Tokyo is all about. If you're after a quick glance at the city, you might wanna look elsewhere. But if you're here to uncover all the amazing stuff Tokyo has to offer, from its hidden corners to its tallest skyscrapers, and you're all about soaking up every bit of that experience, then you're in the right place.

As you flip through these pages, keep an open mind and let Tokyo show you its magic. This city's full of surprises, and with this guide in hand, you're all set to uncover them. Get ready to explore, discover, and maybe even fall head over heels for this incredible place.

So, what are you waiting for? Tokyo's calling your name. Let's make this trip one for the books. Welcome to your Tokyo adventure – it's gonna be epic!

CHAPTER 1
START YOUR TOKYO ADVENTURE

Welcome to the beginning of your unforgettable journey to Tokyo, a city where the future meets tradition in the most dazzling ways. Whether you're dreaming of towering skyscrapers, serene temples, or streets buzzing with life, Tokyo promises an adventure like no other. But before we dive into the heart of this electrifying metropolis, let's figure out the best time to visit, ensuring your trip is packed with the experiences you're yearning for.

1.1 WHEN TO GO

Tokyo, a city with four distinct seasons, each offers a unique palette of experiences. Your perfect timing depends on what you want to see, do, and feel. Let's explore one of the most iconic and sought-after times to visit Tokyo: the Cherry Blossom Spring.

CHERRY BLOSSOM SPRING

Imagine walking through a city, where streets and parks are awash with the soft, enchanting hues of pink and white. Cherry blossom season, or "sakura," as it's called in Japan, is not just a time; it's an experience, deeply ingrained in the Japanese culture and heart.

Timing is Everything: Sakura blooms are famously fleeting, with peak blossoming typically occurring from late March to early April in Tokyo. This magical period is brief, lasting only about a week or two, so timing your visit right is crucial. Keep an eye on the cherry blossom forecasts, which are eagerly anticipated and extensively covered by local media.

Where to Witness the Magic: Some of the best spots to immerse yourself in the sakura spectacle include Ueno Park, with over a thousand trees creating a stunning canopy; the Chidorigafuchi Moat, where you can rent a boat for a serene paddle under the blossoms; and Sumida Park, offering picturesque views with Tokyo Skytree in the background.

Sakura-Themed Events and Foods: Embrace the full sakura experience by partaking in hanami, the traditional practice of flower viewing, where friends and families gather under the blossoms for picnics and parties. Don't miss trying seasonal treats like sakura mochi, a sweet pink rice cake wrapped in a cherry leaf, or sakura-flavored lattes and pastries that pop up in cafes.

What to Bring: The weather can be quite variable, from warm afternoons to chilly evenings. Dress in layers and consider a light, waterproof jacket for those spring showers that help the flowers bloom but might catch you off guard.

Photography Tips: For the aspiring photographers, the soft morning light offers the best natural filter for capturing the sakura's beauty. Experiment with angles – a blanket of petals beneath your feet or a close-up of a single bloom against the urban backdrop can be just as captivating as the wide, sweeping landscapes.

List of Essentials for Cherry Blossom Season:

- Updated Cherry Blossom Forecast App: Stay ahead with real-time updates.
- Portable Picnic Sheet: For those spontaneous hanami moments.
- Camera or Smartphone: Capture the fleeting beauty.
- Layers and a Light Jacket: Be ready for any weather.
- Cash: Some food stalls and markets may not accept cards.
- Reusable Water Bottle: Stay hydrated as you wander.
- Comfortable Walking Shoes: There's a lot of ground to cover.

Tokyo adventure during the cherry blossom season is a choice that offers not just the sight of breathtaking beauty but also a deep dive into the cultural heart of Japan. It's a time of renewal, celebration, and enjoying the fleeting moments of life, encapsulated by the delicate sakura petals dancing in the spring breeze. So, pack your bags with these essentials, and get ready for an experience that will bloom in your memory forever.

As the cherry blossoms blanket the city in pink, many local temples and shrines host special night-time illuminations, allowing visitors to experience these sacred spaces in a different light—literally. The combination of lantern-lit pathways and the soft glow of sakura at night creates a surreal, almost dreamlike atmosphere that's profoundly different from the bustling daytime vibe. This experience highlights the Japanese appreciation for beauty in transience, a concept known as "mono no aware."

Another intriguing element is the impact of sakura on Tokyo's culinary scene. Beyond the usual seasonal treats, many chefs and restaurants across the city incorporate sakura and its leaves into their dishes in innovative ways, creating limited-time menus that offer a taste of spring. From sakura-infused teas and cocktails to delicacies adorned with actual blossoms, these culinary creations provide a sensory exploration of the season.

The cherry blossom season also sparks a wave of creativity in local arts and crafts, with workshops and pop-up markets featuring sakura-themed artworks, handmade jewelry, and traditional crafts. Participating in a craft workshop or visiting these markets not only offers a unique souvenir but also connects travelers with Tokyo's vibrant artisan community, showcasing the city's contemporary creative spirit alongside its ancient traditions.

Moreover, the season influences Tokyo's fashion, with both locals and visitors donning outfits and accessories inspired by the sakura palette. This shift in street fashion adds another layer of color to the city, reflecting the season's aesthetic in everyday life. Observing or even participating in this seasonal change in attire offers insight into the local culture's dynamic nature, where ancient traditions blend seamlessly with modern lifestyle trends.

Lastly, beyond the well-trodden paths, seeking out less famous spots for sakura viewing can lead to discovering Tokyo's hidden neighborhoods and local life. Areas like Yanaka, with its old Tokyo charm, or the residential streets along the Meguro River, offer serene and intimate sakura viewing experiences, away from the crowds. These quiet moments provide a glimpse into the daily rhythms of the city's diverse neighborhoods, where the spectacle of the sakura season is woven into the fabric of local life.

Each of these aspects—night illuminations, seasonal cuisine, arts and crafts, fashion, and hidden viewing spots—enriches the cherry blossom experience in Tokyo, offering travelers a multifaceted understanding of the city during this enchanting season. By delving into these lesser-known experiences, visitors can appreciate the depth of Tokyo's cultural landscape, where the fleeting beauty of sakura leaves a lasting impression on all who witness it.

HOT SUMMER FESTIVALS

Summer in Tokyo is a time when the city truly comes alive, transforming under the heat into a vibrant tableau of festivals that capture the essence of Japanese culture and community spirit. The summer festivals, or "**matsuri**," are not just events; they are experiences that bind the past with the present, offering a glimpse into the soul of Japan.

Tanabata Matsuri: July begins with the Tanabata Festival, a celebration based on a star-crossed lovers' tale, where streets are adorned with colorful streamers. Walking through these whimsically decorated alleys, you can write your own wishes on tanzaku papers and tie them to bamboo, a tradition that's as poetic as the festival's celestial origins.

Sumida River Fireworks Festival: As July edges into its final weeks, the skies above the Sumida River light up with spectacular fireworks. This event, one of the oldest and most famous in Tokyo, draws crowds from all over, painting the night with awe-inspiring bursts of color. It's a moment where the city unites, faces turned skyward, caught in the shared wonder of the display.

Obon Festivals: August is marked by Obon, a Buddhist event for commemorating one's ancestors. It's a period filled with dance, music, and the floating of lanterns on rivers, a sight both beautiful and serene. The Bon Odori dances are a highlight, where everyone is welcome to join in the circular dance moves, celebrating the spirits of ancestors.

Kanda Matsuri and Sanno Matsuri: While these festivals technically occur in alternating years, they're worth planning your trip around. These festivals feature processions of floats, musicians, and dancers winding through the streets, offering a spectacular insight into Tokyo's historical depth and communal joy.

The Essence of Summer Matsuri: Beyond the fireworks, dances, and decorations, summer festivals in Tokyo are about community. They're a time when the city's relentless pace eases into moments of celebration and reflection. Food stalls line the streets, offering everything from grilled squid and yakisoba to sweet, icy kakigori, perfect for the summer heat. It's an experience that engages all senses, from the taste of traditional festival foods to the sound of fireworks and the sight of lantern-lit nights.

Summer in Tokyo is intense, not just because of the heat but also due to the sheer vibrancy of its festivals. Dress lightly, stay hydrated, and immerse yourself in the festivities. Participate in the dances, taste the street food, and let the energy of the city's summer sweep you off your feet.

Another intriguing aspect of Tokyo's summer is the array of niche festivals that celebrate everything from specific foods to contemporary culture. Imagine stumbling upon a festival dedicated entirely to ramen, where you can taste different regional varieties under one roof, or a high-energy dance music festival that takes over a part of the city with DJs and live performances. These events showcase Tokyo's ability to blend tradition with modernity, offering something for everyone.

The Edo Noren market near Ryogoku becomes a hub of activity in summer, where you can explore Tokyo's sumo culture up close. This area, steeped in the history of sumo wrestling, offers a unique insight into one of Japan's oldest sports, complete with sumo stables and shops selling related merchandise. It's a different kind of festival atmosphere, one that celebrates sports and history together.

In the heat of summer, Tokyo's many gardens and parks transform into escapes from the urban rush, with some hosting evening illuminations or night markets. These events are perfect for those looking to enjoy the outdoors without the daytime heat. The gardens of Rikugien and the historical Kiyosumi Teien open their doors for night-time strolls, providing a tranquil atmosphere where you can admire the illuminated landscapes and sometimes even catch a traditional tea ceremony in progress.

The resurgence of traditional Japanese crafts during festival times offers a hands-on experience for visitors interested in more than just sightseeing. Workshops and pop-up stalls become common sights, where you can try your hand at creating your own indigo-dyed fabrics, pottery, or join in a lantern-making session.

COLORFUL AUTUMN EATS

As the heat of summer fades, giving way to the crisp, cool air of autumn, Tokyo's culinary scene undergoes a transformation as well. This is when the city's food becomes a celebration of the harvest, a testament to the Japanese reverence for nature and the changing seasons.

- **Seasonal Ingredients at Their Peak**: Autumn introduces a bounty of seasonal ingredients that find their way into Tokyo's culinary repertoire. **Sweet potatoes, chestnuts**, and **pumpkins** become the stars of both sweet and savory dishes, each ingredient reflecting the season's essence. Restaurants and street vendors alike showcase these ingredients, offering everything from roasted chestnuts that warm your hands and heart to sweet potato treats that are as delightful to the eyes as they are to the taste.
- **Mushroom Magic**: Another autumn highlight is the variety of mushrooms that flood the markets. From the delicate shimeji to the hearty matsutake, mushrooms are celebrated in Japanese cuisine for their depth of flavor. They're featured in everything from simple grilled dishes, where their natural flavors shine, to intricate soups and broths that warm you from the inside out on a crisp autumn day.
- **The Art of Autumn Sweets:** Tokyo's sweet scene also gets an autumn makeover, with wagashi (traditional Japanese sweets) taking center stage. Crafted to mimic the season's colors and motifs, these sweets are not just a treat for the palate but a feast for the eyes. Imagine biting into a delicate sweet shaped like a maple leaf or savoring a mochi filled with sweet bean paste, each bite a reflection of autumn's fleeting beauty.
- **Seasonal Seafood Delights**: Autumn also means an abundance of seafood, with Pacific saury (sanma), salmon, and oysters topping the list of seasonal catches. Grilled sanma, served with a squeeze of sudachi lime, is a simple yet profound culinary experience, embodying the essence of autumn's bounty.

- **Autumn Festivals and Food Fairs:** Beyond the daily dishes, autumn is also a time for food-focused festivals and fairs, where you can sample a wide array of seasonal delicacies in one place. From sweet potato festivals to celebrations dedicated to sake, which is often brewed in the fall, these events offer a glimpse into Japan's rich culinary traditions and the communal spirit of enjoying the season's harvest together.

Exploring Tokyo in autumn is an invitation to experience the harmony between nature and cuisine, a journey where each meal is a moment to savor, and every bite tells the story of the season.

WINTER LIGHTS AND NEW YEAR

Illuminations to Light Up the Night: As the days shorten and the nights draw in, Tokyo transforms into a wonderland of lights. From November through February, districts across the city compete in splendor, with LED displays that range from elegant white lights draped over trees to elaborate themes that tell a story or evoke the wonders of nature. Areas like Roppongi, Shibuya, and Marunouchi are just a few hotspots where the light shows create a magical atmosphere, inviting couples, families, and friends to stroll through these luminous landscapes, often with a hot drink in hand to ward off the chill.

The Warmth of Winter Cuisine: Winter is also a time when Tokyo's cuisine takes on a heartier, warming character. Street vendors and restaurants alike serve up soul-warming fare, from steaming bowls of ramen and hot pots (nabe) that bring people together around a simmering pot, to sweet potatoes roasted on open fires and sold by street vendors, their smoky aroma filling the cold air. It's a season to indulge in comfort foods that not only warm the body but also comfort the soul.

New Year Traditions: As December wanes, Tokyo's attention turns to the New Year, or "Shogatsu," a time rich with tradition and reflection. It's a period marked by a series of rituals and customs, from the ringing of temple bells at midnight, which symbolize the letting go of the past year's woes, to the first shrine visit of the year, known as "hatsumode." Temples and shrines across the city, such as the Meiji Shrine and Asakusa's Senso-ji, become focal points of celebration, drawing millions who come to pray for good fortune, health, and happiness in the year ahead.

Experiencing Osechi-ryori: No New Year celebration would be complete without "osechi-ryori," traditional New Year's cuisine that is both a feast for the eyes and a culinary exploration of Japanese flavors. These bento-like boxes are filled with an assortment of dishes, each symbolizing different wishes for the new year, such as health, fertility, and prosperity. Experiencing osechi-ryori offers a unique insight into Japanese culture and traditions, making it a must-try for anyone visiting Tokyo during this season.

First Sunrise of the Year: Another deeply moving experience is witnessing the first sunrise of the year, or "hatsuhinode." It's a moment of profound beauty and significance, symbolizing renewal and hope. Many gather at spots known for their sunrise views, such as the seaside at Odaiba or the heights of Mount Takao, to share in this moment of collective joy and anticipation for the year to come.

Winter in Tokyo is a season of contrast and celebration, where the cold is countered by the warmth of festive lights, hearty meals, and the spirit of the New Year. It's a time when the city offers not just sights to behold but experiences that touch the heart, drawing visitors into the communal embrace of Tokyo's winter wonderland.

Another aspect that often goes unnoticed is the winter food markets that pop up around the city. These markets are a foodie's paradise, offering an array of seasonal produce, freshly prepared street food, and unique local delicacies that are best enjoyed in the crisp winter air. They provide a perfect opportunity to mingle with locals and experience the city's vibrant food culture firsthand.

Winter also brings with it the chance to see Tokyo dressed in snow. While snowfall in Tokyo is rare, when it does happen, it transforms the city into a picturesque wonderland. Iconic spots like the Imperial Palace, Ueno Park, and the Meiji Shrine draped in snow offer a once-in-a-lifetime photography opportunity, presenting a side of Tokyo that's markedly different from its usual bustling persona.

For those interested in winter sports, Tokyo's proximity to several ski resorts is often overlooked. Day trips to nearby mountains for skiing or snowboarding are easily doable, offering the thrill of winter sports against the backdrop of Japan's stunning natural beauty. It's a side adventure that combines the urban exploration of Tokyo with the excitement of the Japanese Alps.

The end of the year in Tokyo is marked by "bonenkai" parties, or year-forgetting parties, where friends and colleagues gather to bid farewell to the year's troubles and look forward to the new year. Participating in or observing these gatherings offers insight into Japanese work culture and the importance of camaraderie and collective reflection as the year comes to a close.

Each of these experiences adds layers to the winter adventure in Tokyo, offering paths less traveled that reveal the city's multifaceted personality.

1.2 TOKYO BASICS

Tokyo is more than just a city; it's a constellation of districts, each with its own personality, rhythm, and secrets waiting to be discovered.

GETTING YOUR BEARINGS: CITY LAYOUT

Central Tokyo and the Yamanote Line: Imagine Tokyo as a giant circle with the Yamanote train line running looped within it. This line is your golden compass, connecting major districts and serving as a reliable reference point for navigating the city. Central Tokyo is inside this loop, housing key areas like Shibuya, Shinjuku, and Harajuku, each a universe unto itself with distinct vibes and attractions.

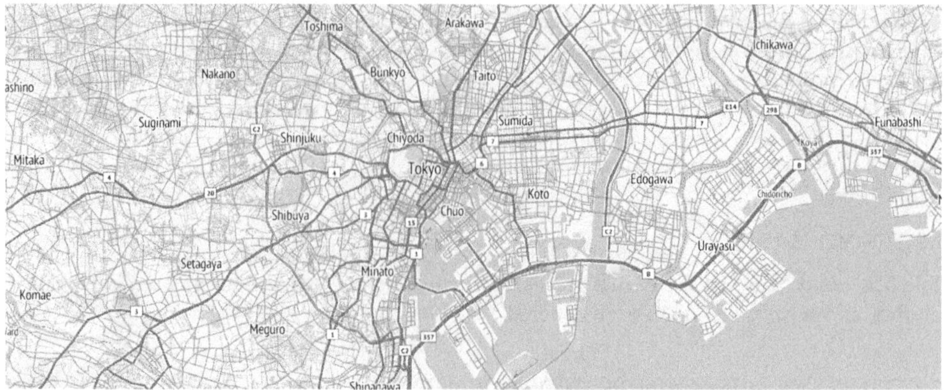

The Wards: Tokyo is divided into 23 special wards, each functioning almost as an individual city. Some, like Minato, Chiyoda, and Shibuya, are bustling hubs of activity, while others, such as Setagaya or Taito, offer a glimpse into Tokyo's quieter, more laid-back side. Knowing which ward you're in helps you grasp the city's immense scale and the diverse experiences each area offers.

Beyond Central Tokyo: Stretching out from the Yamanote circle are other fascinating areas, each with its own charm. Places like Nakano, known for its otaku culture, and Odaiba, a futuristic waterfront district, are easily accessible and provide a fuller picture of Tokyo's diversity. The further you venture, the more you uncover Tokyo's contrasts, from skyscraper-studded landscapes to tranquil, suburban neighborhoods.

Rivers and Green Spaces: Tokyo's rivers, such as the Sumida River, and its green spaces, like the Imperial Palace Gardens, provide natural waypoints and a respite from the urban rush. These areas are not just beautiful oases; they're also key landmarks that help you orient yourself within the city's vast expanse.

Understanding Addresses: Tokyo's address system can be perplexing, with numbers often based on the order buildings were constructed rather than their location on a street. While this might seem confusing, focusing on landmarks, subway stations, and ward names is a more intuitive way to find your way around. Plus, Tokyoites are generally helpful, so asking for directions becomes a chance to interact and maybe even discover a local's favorite spot.

Places like Asakusa, with its ancient temple Senso-ji, sit comfortably amid the buzz of modern businesses, offering a live walkthrough of Tokyo's transformation from the Edo period to today.

Then there's the concept of "shitamachi" and "yamanote." Historically, Tokyo was divided into these two social classes, with shitamachi (literally "low city") areas like Ueno and Asakusa being the heart of old Tokyo where merchants and artisans lived. Yamanote ("high city"), encompassing areas like Shibuya and Shinjuku, was traditionally home to the nobility and samurai. This division has evolved, but exploring these areas can give you a taste of Tokyo's social layers and historical depth.

Another intriguing tidbit is how natural disasters have shaped Tokyo's layout. Following the great Kanto earthquake in 1923 and the bombings in World War II, Tokyo had to be extensively rebuilt. This led to a city that's a mix of meticulous planning in some areas and organic, somewhat chaotic growth in others. This blend gives Tokyo its unique character, where ultra-modern buildings stand next to narrow lanes lined with tiny, traditional shops.

Relationship with water is another layer to its geography. The city is interlaced with rivers and canals, remnants of a time when goods were transported by boat. The Sumida River, flanked by cherry blossoms, not only offers a stunning scenic route but also tells the tale of Tokyo's trade and strategic defense history. The many bridges crossing over the Sumida are not just functional; they're historical markers, each with its own story.

Green spaces, like the vast Yoyogi Park and the Imperial Palace Gardens, are not accidental. They're part of Tokyo's conscious effort to balance its urban intensity with nature's tranquility. These areas serve as the city's lungs, offering not just recreational space but also a sanctuary for biodiversity. They're a testament to Tokyo's philosophy of coexisting with nature, amidst the concrete jungle.

DAYTIME VIBES

As the sun rises, Tokyo awakens with a gentle hum, gradually building to the bustling energy of day. Streets come alive with locals and visitors alike, each on their own quest.

Exploring Historic Sites and Parks: The daylight hours are perfect for visiting Tokyo's iconic temples, shrines, and gardens. The serene atmosphere of Meiji Shrine, juxtaposed with the youthful energy of Harajuku just nearby, offers a fascinating glimpse into Tokyo's cultural duality.

Shopping and Urban Exploration: Daytime is ideal for shopping, from the high-end boutiques of Ginza to the electronic wonderland of Akihabara. It's also the best time to explore neighborhoods, each with its own character, from the fashion-forward streets of Shibuya to the quaint lanes of Yanaka.

Culinary Adventures: Tokyo's culinary scene shines brightly by day. Morning markets, like Tsukiji's outer market, offer fresh seafood, while countless cafes, ramen shops, and izakayas prepare for the lunchtime rush, providing endless options to savor Tokyo's gastronomic delights.

NIGHTTIME LIGHTS

As dusk falls, Tokyo dons a new persona, illuminated by the neon glow of its skyscrapers and bustling nightlife. The city transforms into a canvas of light, inviting a different kind of exploration.

Illuminated Landmarks and Cityscapes: Tokyo Tower, Skytree, and the Rainbow Bridge offer breathtaking views against the night sky. Districts like Shinjuku and Roppongi become stages for light shows that dazzle the senses.

Evening Entertainment and Dining: Nightlife in Tokyo ranges from the tranquil (sake tasting in quiet bars) to the electric (clubbing in Shibuya). Dining options also transform, with yakitori stalls and late-night ramen joints offering a taste of Tokyo's after-hours food culture.

Cultural Experiences: Evening is a time for cultural immersion, whether attending a traditional kabuki performance, exploring the night markets of Odaiba, or joining a local festival. It's when the city's heart beats loudest, showcasing its love for celebration and community.

List of Must-Experience Day and Night Activities:

Day: Visit the Imperial Palace Gardens, shop in Omotesando, explore the Edo-Tokyo Museum, and enjoy sushi for lunch.

Night: View the city from Mori Tower's observation deck, dine in Piss Alley, experience karaoke in Shinjuku, and stroll through Shibuya's neon-lit streets.

Tokyo's dual identity, marked by the contrast between its daytime serenity and nighttime vibrancy, offers endless possibilities for discovery.

PACKING FOR THE WEATHER

Spring (March to May): Spring in Tokyo is mild and pleasant, but with a chance of rain. Pack layers—a mix of light jackets, sweaters, and comfortable walking shoes. Don't forget an umbrella or a waterproof jacket for those sudden spring showers. This is also cherry blossom season, so bring a picnic sheet if you plan on joining the hanami festivities.

Summer (June to August): Tokyo summers are hot and humid. Lightweight and breathable clothing will be your best friend. Think cotton shirts, shorts, and open-toed sandals. Sun protection is a must—sunglasses, a wide-brimmed hat, and sunscreen are essential. Also, a hand fan or a portable fan can be a lifesaver when exploring the city.

Autumn (September to November): Autumn brings cooler temperatures and the beauty of changing leaves. Packing similar to spring—layers are key. A comfortable sweater, light scarves, and a versatile jacket should suffice. Comfortable walking shoes are essential for exploring parks and gardens adorned with autumn foliage.

Winter (December to February): Winters in Tokyo can be cold, with temperatures occasionally dropping near freezing. A warm coat, scarves, gloves, and a hat are necessary. Consider thermal underlayers for extra warmth on colder days. While snow is rare in the city, waterproof shoes are a good idea in case you encounter a snowy day or plan to visit nearby snowy regions.

Year-Round Essentials:

Comfortable Footwear: Regardless of the season, you'll be walking a lot. Comfortable shoes are a must.

Portable Charger: With all the photos you'll be taking and maps you'll be using, your phone's battery will drain quickly.

Reusable Water Bottle: Stay hydrated as you explore. Tokyo has many public water fountains where you can refill your bottle.

Eco Bag: Many shops charge for plastic bags. Carry an eco-friendly tote for your purchases.

Packing for Tokyo isn't just about preparing for the weather; it's about gearing up for an adventure in a city that's constantly in motion. Each season in Tokyo offers a unique palette of experiences, from the serene beauty of cherry blossoms to the vibrant energy of summer festivals, the poetic charm of autumn leaves, and the crisp air of winter illuminations. By packing smartly, you ensure that no matter what the weather throws your way, you're ready to embrace every moment, every sight, and every new discovery that Tokyo has to offer.

So, as you lay out your suitcase, remember that you're not just packing clothes and gadgets —you're preparing for an unforgettable journey into the heart of one of the world's most fascinating cities. With each item you pack, you're one step closer to the adventures that await you in Tokyo, a city that promises endless exploration and surprises around every corner.

1.3 BUDGETING YOUR TRIP

Exploring Tokyo doesn't have to drain your wallet. With some savvy planning and insider tips, you can soak up the city's vibrant culture without splurging.

SAVING MONEY IN TOKYO

Travel Smart with Passes: Tokyo's public transport network is your gateway to the city. Save a bundle with a PASMO or Suica card, rechargeable smart cards for all your transport needs. For tourists, the Tokyo Subway Ticket offers unlimited rides on the metro and Toei lines for up to 72 hours, a steal for anyone looking to crisscross the city.

Dine Like a Local: Tokyo's culinary scene offers delights at every price point. Sidestep the pricey restaurants in favor of conveyor belt sushi spots, ramen shops, and the revered konbini (convenience stores) for delicious, budget-friendly meals. Don't miss out on the standing sushi bars and izakayas where locals flock. Here, the dishes are delectable, and the prices are gentle on your wallet.

Free Attractions Galore: Tokyo is peppered with experiences that cost nothing but are rich in memories. Stroll through the Imperial Palace East Gardens, lose yourself in the hustle of Tsukiji Outer Market, or witness the iconic Shibuya crossing. Temples and shrines like Senso-ji offer a glimpse into Tokyo's soul without demanding a yen for entry.

Shop Wisely: Shopping in Tokyo can be an adventure in itself. Hunt for unique finds in the city's numerous 100-yen shops, where souvenirs, snacks, and household items come at astonishingly low prices. Explore the thrift shops in Koenji or Shimokitazawa for vintage clothing at a fraction of the cost.

Stay Smart: Accommodation in Tokyo spans the spectrum from luxury hotels to unique capsule hostels. Save significantly by staying in capsule hotels, guesthouses, or hostels. Booking platforms often offer last-minute deals, and staying a little outside the city center can dramatically lower costs without sacrificing convenience, thanks to Tokyo's efficient public transport.

Enjoy Nature's Bounty: Tokyo's parks and gardens provide serene escapes from the urban frenzy at zero cost. Whether it's the expansive Yoyogi Park or the picturesque Shinjuku Gyoen, nature's splendor in Tokyo is yours to enjoy without opening your wallet.

Cultural Experiences for Free: Look out for cultural festivals and local events happening around the city. From sumo practice viewing in Ryogoku to contemporary art in Roppongi, thes

Beyond the basic tips, there are layers of insider knowledge that can help you dive deeper into Tokyo's culture without splurging. For instance, tapping into the city's vibrant scene of free workshops and events often hosted in local community centers or libraries can offer unique insights into traditional crafts and contemporary arts. These sessions not only enrich your travel experience but also connect you with locals and other travelers.

Night markets and local festivals, which aren't always highlighted in mainstream travel guides, are treasure troves of affordable eats and entertainment. Keep an eye on local district websites or community bulletin boards for announcements. Participating in these community events can give you a taste of Tokyo's local flavors and festivities at a fraction of the cost.

For those looking to explore Tokyo's natural landscapes, consider day trips to nearby mountains or islands like Mount Takao or the Izu Islands. Accessible by local trains or ferries, these getaways offer hiking, hot springs, and beaches, providing a break from the city's pace at little to no cost.

Leveraging Tokyo's extensive network of bike rentals is another underutilized way to save on transport while gaining a new perspective on the city. Cycling through neighborhoods gives you the flexibility to explore at your own pace, discovering hidden alleys, local eateries, and picturesque spots away from the tourist crowds.

Embracing Tokyo's culture of sharing and exchange can lead to unexpected savings. Platforms and social media groups dedicated to expats and travelers often have tips, meet-ups, and even swap events for books, clothes, and more. Engaging with these communities can not only help stretch your yen but also enrich your travel experience with new friendships and local insights.

CASH OR CARD? SPENDING TIPS

Cash is King: Despite its futuristic façade, Tokyo has a surprising preference for cash transactions, especially in smaller restaurants, market stalls, and some shops. Having cash on hand isn't just convenient—it's often necessary. Withdraw yen from ATMs at 7-Eleven or Japan Post Bank, known for their foreign card-friendly services. Remember, carrying cash is safe in Tokyo, a city with one of the lowest crime rates.

Cards for Bigger Buys: For larger purchases, hotel stays, or shopping in department stores and upscale boutiques, credit cards are widely accepted. Visa and Mastercard are the most commonly accepted, with American Express a close third. Always have a backup payment method, as not all places accept cards, and international transactions can sometimes trigger fraud alerts.

Tapping Into the Future: For a seamless experience, load your Suica or Pasmo transport card with cash. These cards are lifesavers for public transportation and can also be used for small purchases at convenience stores, vending machines, and even some restaurants. It's like having a magic wand in your pocket that covers both your travel and snack needs.

Avoiding Fees: Keep an eye on transaction fees. Using your card can sometimes incur international charges, so it's wise to check with your bank before you travel. When withdrawing cash, doing so in larger amounts can minimize fees charged by ATMs.

Budget Apps: To keep a handle on your spending, consider using a budget tracking app. Many apps can convert your expenses into your home currency in real-time, helping you stay aware of how much you're really spending.

Emergency Cash: Always keep a small reserve of cash hidden away for unexpected situations. Whether it's a taxi ride back to your lodging after the last train or a must-have souvenir from a cash-only vendor, this emergency stash can be a day-saver.

For starters, many travelers don't realize that while credit card acceptance is growing, some specific types of businesses, especially traditional ones like small bathhouses, local bars, or mom-and-pop eateries, might still operate on a cash-only basis. This isn't just about tradition; it's about keeping costs down by avoiding card transaction fees, which can be particularly high for small businesses.

Another point to consider is the emerging trend of QR code payments in Tokyo. Apps like PayPay, Line Pay, and others are becoming increasingly popular for cashless transactions, even among smaller vendors. While these platforms are fantastic for locals, they can be tricky for travelers due to registration requirements, including a Japanese phone number. However, witnessing their use is a peek into Tokyo's fast-evolving digital payment scene.

For those late-night adventures or early morning starts, knowing that ATMs in Japan have operating hours can save you from being caught without cash. Not all ATMs operate 24/7, and even those within convenience stores might have restrictions, especially on weekends and national holidays. Planning your cash withdrawals accordingly can avoid any unnecessary stress.

The etiquette of handling money in Tokyo is an experience in itself. When making purchases, you'll notice that cash and cards are usually placed on a small tray rather than handed directly to the cashier. This practice respects privacy and minimizes physical contact, reflecting the subtle courtesies that underpin daily life in Tokyo.

FINDING DEALS AND PASSES

Travel Smart with Transport Passes: The labyrinth of Tokyo's public transport system is your gateway to exploration. Arm yourself with a PASMO or Suica card, not just for convenience but for savings too. For visitors, the Tokyo Subway Ticket is a goldmine, offering unlimited travel on all Tokyo Metro and Toei Subway lines for 24, 48, or 72 hours. Imagine the freedom to roam the city without the worry of transport costs adding up.

Dive into Culture with Discount Passes: Tokyo's rich tapestry of museums, gardens, and historic sites can be accessed with various discount passes. The Grutto Pass, for example, offers entry to 95 facilities over two months at a fraction of the cost. It's like having a VIP pass to Tokyo's cultural heart, from art galleries to science museums, without the hefty price tag.

Stay Connected for Less: Staying online in Tokyo is essential, but roaming charges can be a nightmare. Enter pocket Wi-Fi rental services and tourist SIM cards, available at airports and major train stations. Book these online in advance to snag early bird discounts, ensuring you're always connected to navigate the city, translate menus, or post real-time updates of your adventure, all without the fear of coming home to a scary phone bill.

Accommodation Hacks: Beyond the usual hotel booking sites, consider unique lodging options like capsule hotels, guesthouses, or even short-term apartment rentals. Websites like Airbnb or local equivalents offer competitive rates, especially if you're staying longer. Pro tip: Look for accommodations offering "weekly mansion" rates for extended stays, blending comfort with affordability.

Eat, Drink, Save: Tokyo's culinary scene can be surprisingly affordable if you know where to look. Lunch sets in restaurants offer the same high-quality cuisine as dinner but at a fraction of the cost. Also, visiting izakayas (Japanese pubs) during "happy hour" can land you great deals on food and drink, perfect for tasting a variety of Japanese dishes without the hefty price tag.

Experience More for Less: Keep an eye out for free community events, workshops, and local festivals. These can offer immersive cultural experiences—from pottery classes to traditional tea ceremonies—often just for the cost of materials. Plus, exploring Tokyo's parks, temples, and historic neighborhoods costs nothing but can yield rich memories and insights into Japanese life.

Tapping into the "last-minute" market can yield unexpected savings, especially for accommodations and entertainment. Websites and apps catering to the Japanese market often feature last-minute deals for hotels, traditional inns, and even tickets to shows or sports events. This approach requires a bit of flexibility but can lead to luxurious experiences at a fraction of the cost.

Here's a quick list of tips for finding deals and passes in Tokyo:

- Look for free admission days at museums and galleries.
- Utilize last-minute booking apps for accommodations and entertainment.
- Explore multi-use transport passes for unlimited travel.
- Check out lunch specials at high-end restaurants for gourmet dining without the gourmet price tag.
- Attend free local festivals and workshops for cultural immersion.
- Use city-wide Wi-Fi spots to save on data charges.
- Shop at 100-yen stores for souvenirs and essentials.
- Eat at standing restaurants for quick, delicious, and affordable meals.
- Drink at izakayas with nomihodai (all-you-can-drink) deals for a budget-friendly night out.
- Rent a bicycle to explore neighborhoods cheaply and at your own pace.

1.4 STAYING ONLINE

INTERNET EVERYWHERE: WI-FI AND SIMS

Tokyo, a city that's as wired as it is vast, offers a plethora of options to keep you connected. The city understands that in this day and age, the internet is as vital as the air we breathe, especially for savvy travelers eager to experience Tokyo's endless wonders.

Wi-Fi Connectivity in Tokyo is surprisingly accessible. From the moment you step off the plane, you're greeted with a network of free Wi-Fi hotspots covering airports, major train stations, cafes, and even some public parks. Tokyo Metro stations offer free Wi-Fi, perfect for checking directions or your next destination as you move around the city. For those leisurely café breaks, spots like Starbucks and Tully's not only offer a caffeine fix but also free internet, though you might need to sign up first.

However, relying solely on public Wi-Fi can be hit or miss, with varying speeds and the hassle of constantly logging in at different spots. That's where Portable Wi-Fi Routers and Tourist SIM Cards come into play, offering a seamless, always-on connection.

Portable Wi-Fi Routers are a traveler's best friend, providing high-speed internet wherever you go, from the neon-lit streets of Shinjuku to the serene gardens of the Imperial Palace. Rental shops are conveniently located at airports and major train stations, offering daily rates that are budget-friendly. The beauty of a portable router is that multiple devices can connect, making it a perfect option for groups or families.

Tourist SIM Cards, on the other hand, offer a direct line to the digital world through your smartphone. Available for purchase at airports, electronic stores, and even some convenience stores, these SIM cards come with a variety of data plans to suit your needs, from short stays to longer explorations. The setup is straightforward, and you're immediately granted access to high-speed internet, making every search, post, and stream as smooth as the bullet train.

Both options have their perks, but the choice boils down to your specific needs. Are you a solo adventurer who's content with a SIM card, or are you leading a squad of explorers who'd benefit from a Wi-Fi router's group connectivity?

Staying online in Tokyo allows you to dive deep into the city's heart, uncovering not just the landmarks but also the stories, the local hangouts, and the spontaneous experiences that define the Tokyo journey.

You're exploring the historic alleys of Asakusa, and a sudden craving for ramen hits. With a few taps on your device, you discover a hidden gem that's not just any ramen shop but one that's been praised by locals for its rich, flavorful broth and perfectly chewy noodles. Or perhaps you find yourself captivated by the serene beauty of the Meiji Shrine, and you're curious about its history. Within seconds, you're reading about its significance, deepening your appreciation for the site you're visiting.

But it's not just about convenience. Staying connected also opens up a world of social interaction. Sharing your experiences in real time, whether it's through a live video of the bustling Shibuya Crossing or a quick story of your serene morning in the Imperial Palace Gardens, lets you bring your friends and followers along for the ride. It's a way to document your journey, capturing moments of awe, wonder, and the sheer joy of discovery.

Moreover, the digital connection offers a safety net. Access to maps and transportation schedules means you're never truly lost, and the ability to reach out for help or advice is always in your pocket. It's the reassurance that, in a city as vast and as vibrant as Tokyo, you're never alone.

MUST-HAVE APPS FOR TOKYO

Walking the vibrant streets, every app has a new lens through which to view the city's endless layers.

Navigation Apps: Navigating Tokyo's intricate transport system feels like a breeze with the right app. One that combines real-time transit schedules, station maps, and route options across all forms of public transport, from the shinkansen to local buses, becomes indispensable. It guides you step by step, ensuring you're always on the fastest or most efficient path to your next destination.

Translation Tools: Face-to-face with a menu in a cozy, backstreet izakaya, a translation app becomes your culinary guide, turning bewildering characters into a list of delicious possibilities. It's not just about food; it's about unlocking conversations, understanding directions, and diving into the culture without the language barrier holding you back.

Cultural Insight Apps: Apps that offer insights into Tokyo's rich history and cultural landmarks turn your exploration into a story-filled journey. Picture standing before an ancient temple or a modern architectural marvel, and with a tap, you're immersed in its history, significance, and the stories that make it alive.

Payment and Shopping Apps: In a city where cash was once king, mobile payment apps now open up a world of convenience. They're not just for buying that perfect souvenir or paying for a meal but also for discovering deals, promotions, and even hidden shopping gems recommended by locals.

Social Connection Apps: These apps do more than help you stay in touch; they connect you with fellow travelers and locals. Joining a local event, finding a meetup, or even seeking recommendations becomes a shared adventure, adding unexpected turns and new friends to your Tokyo tale.

Beyond the essential apps for navigation, translation, and cultural insights, there are hidden digital gems that cater to niche interests and provide access to local events, exclusive deals, and community gatherings.

For the foodies, apps that specialize in ramen or sushi locations offer detailed reviews and rankings from locals, guiding you to the best spots that might not even have a sign in English. Art and design enthusiasts can find apps that map out galleries, pop-up art events, and design shops, turning the city into a treasure hunt for creativity.

Photography apps with geotagged photos can help you discover and capture Tokyo's most Instagrammable spots, from hidden alleys lit by paper lanterns to the perfect viewpoint for capturing the sprawling cityscape. Fitness enthusiasts might enjoy apps that track running routes or public sports facilities, allowing for a workout with a view or a chance to join a local sports club for a game.

Additionally, environmental apps provide information on recycling centers and eco-friendly stores, appealing to the eco-conscious traveler looking to maintain a green lifestyle while exploring Tokyo.

- Foodie apps for discovering local eateries
- Art and design event locators
- Photography location guides
- Fitness and outdoor activity trackers
- Environmental and sustainability resources

These specialized apps not only enhance your Tokyo experience but also connect you with like-minded communities, whether you're a food lover, art aficionado, fitness fanatic, or eco-warrior.

SHARING YOUR TRIP ON SOCIAL MEDIA

In the whirlwind of Tokyo's landscapes, from the serene to the electrifying, each moment holds the potential to be captured, curated, and shared. But sharing your Tokyo journey on social media isn't merely about posting photos or updates; it's about telling a story, your story, set against the backdrop of one of the world's most dynamic cities.

Crafting Your Narrative: Tokyo offers a kaleidoscope of experiences. Whether it's the quiet contemplation of a Zen garden, the frenzy of Shibuya's crossing, or the culinary ballet in a tiny sushi bar, each experience contributes to the narrative of your adventure. When sharing, think about the story you want to tell. Is it one of discovery, of culinary exploits, or perhaps of cultural immersion? Let your posts weave together to tell this tale, offering your audience a window into your journey and the soul of Tokyo.

Visual Storytelling: In Tokyo, every corner offers a visual feast, from the neon-lit nights to the delicate hues of cherry blossoms. Utilizing the power of visuals on platforms like Instagram or Pinterest can capture the essence of your experiences. Experiment with angles, filters, and captions to add depth to your images, making each post not just a photo but a story in itself. Remember, the best shots are those that capture not just a place but a moment, an emotion that Tokyo evokes in you.

Engaging with Your Audience: Sharing your trip is also about interaction. Use your posts to ask questions, share insights, or invite recommendations. It's a way to not only inform but also connect and engage with your followers, turning your solo journey into a shared adventure. Platforms like Twitter or Facebook are excellent for sparking conversations, whether it's about the best ramen spots or tips for navigating Tokyo's subway maze.

Responsible Sharing: In the excitement of sharing, it's crucial to remember the etiquette of social media. Respect privacy, both yours and others', and be mindful of cultural sensitivities, especially when capturing and sharing images of people or religious sites. Tokyo, with its blend of the sacred and the profane, the traditional and the hyper-modern, demands a nuanced approach to what and how you share.

Reflecting and Inspiring: Ultimately, sharing your Tokyo trip on social media serves a dual purpose: it allows you to reflect on and curate your experiences, creating a digital diary that you can look back on. But perhaps more importantly, it inspires others, kindling in them the desire to explore, to see Tokyo through their eyes, and to create their own narratives in this ever-changing city.

Some fresh angles and ideas to elevate your social media game and share your Tokyo story in a way that's both authentic and captivating:

Hyper-lapse Videos of Busy Crosswalks: Capture the energy of Tokyo's bustling streets, like Shibuya Crossing, through hyper-lapse videos. These sped-up clips not only highlight the city's dynamic pace but also add a cool, artistic twist to your feed.

Food Stories with a Twist: Instead of just snapping pics of your meals, share stories or reels that showcase the entire experience, from entering the tiny ramen shop to watching your dish being prepared right in front of you. It's about the journey, not just the destination.

Interactive Polls and Q&As: Engage your audience with polls about which sights to see next or Q&A sessions sharing insights about life in Tokyo. It turns your trip into a shared adventure with your followers.

Before-and-After Edits: Show off your editing skills and the power of perspective by posting before-and-after shots of a scene or landmark. It's a great way to share photography tips and tricks with your followers.

Soundscapes of the City: Record and share the sounds of Tokyo, from the melodies of street performers in Ueno Park to the bustling noise of Tsukiji Fish Market. It adds an auditory layer to your visual storytelling.

Local Interactions: With consent, share moments of interaction with locals, whether it's a barista teaching you a Japanese phrase or a street artist sharing their story. These encounters add depth and personal connection to your journey.

Incorporating these elements into your social media strategy not only enriches your storytelling but also paints a fuller, more vibrant picture of Tokyo for your audience.

1.5 KEEPING SAFE

STAYING OUT OF TROUBLE

Tokyo, a city that respects rules and manners, offers a safe haven for travelers. Yet, understanding and adhering to its unspoken codes and regulations is key to a seamless experience. Navigating this metropolis, where tradition meets hyper-modernity, requires a blend of respect, awareness, and common sense.

Respect Local Customs and Etiquette: Tokyo thrives on respect. Simple gestures, such as bowing slightly in thanks, removing your shoes before entering someone's home or certain traditional establishments, and speaking softly on public transport, resonate deeply with the local culture. It's about blending in, not standing out, ensuring your actions reflect sensitivity towards Tokyo's societal norms.

Mind the Rules: Tokyo's orderliness is no accident. It's maintained through adherence to rules, from following pedestrian traffic on sidewalks and escalators to observing no-smoking zones on streets. Even seemingly minor infractions, like littering or jaywalking, can attract unwanted attention and disrupt the harmony that Tokyo so cherishes.

Nightlife Navigation: Tokyo's nightlife, as vibrant and enticing as it may be, demands a cautious approach. Stick to well-lit, populated areas and be wary of invitation-only bars or clubs, where you might face unexpectedly high bills. Establishing a clear understanding of prices and services beforehand can avert any misunderstandings or uncomfortable situations.

Stay Informed: Keeping abreast of local news and advisories, especially regarding natural events like earthquakes or typhoons, is crucial. Tokyo is well-prepared for such occurrences, and knowing the drill can help you stay calm and safe. Mobile apps and community alerts can provide real-time updates and instructions.

Personal Belongings and Scams: While Tokyo is remarkably safe regarding personal security, it's wise to keep an eye on your belongings in crowded places. Scams are rare, but staying alert to common tourist traps, particularly in bustling tourist areas, is always a good practice.

Navigating Tokyo with an awareness of these facets not only ensures your safety but also enhances your enjoyment of the city. It's about experiencing the boundless wonders of Tokyo while maintaining a harmonious presence within its rhythm.

There are unique aspects of Tokyo's environment and daily life that, when understood, can significantly enhance your safety and overall experience in the city.

Understanding Earthquake Preparedness: Tokyo is in an earthquake-prone area. Familiarize yourself with the basic safety measures, like ducking under a sturdy table during a quake and knowing the evacuation routes of places you're staying in or visiting.

Allergen Awareness in Food: With the rich culinary scene, being clear about any food allergies is crucial. Learn the Japanese words for your specific allergens to avoid any mix-ups when ordering food.

Navigating with Respect in Religious Places: When visiting temples or shrines, observing quiet and following posted instructions for rituals or photography ensures you're not inadvertently disrespectful.

Dealing with Crowds: Tokyo can get incredibly crowded, especially during rush hours and festivals. Keeping your belongings secure and being mindful of personal space helps navigate these situations smoothly.

Cycling Rules: If you decide to rent a bike, knowing Tokyo's cycling laws is key. Cycling on sidewalks is allowed only where indicated, and parking bikes in non-designated areas can lead to them being impounded.

Emergency Contacts: Have a list of emergency contacts, including the local embassy or consulate, emergency services, and a local contact point like your hotel's front desk, saved in your phone.

Weather Readiness: Sudden weather changes, especially during typhoon season, can impact travel plans. Apps that provide local weather alerts help you stay prepared and adjust your plans accordingly.

WHERE TO GET HELP

Tokyo, a city that prides itself on its order, safety, and the unwavering kindness of its people, offers several lifelines should you find yourself in need of assistance. Whether it's navigating the intricate subway system, seeking medical attention, or dealing with lost items, Tokyo has structures in place to guide you back to safety.

Koban – The Neighborhood Police Box: Scattered across Tokyo, these small police stations are beacons of assistance, offering help with directions, lost and found items, and immediate safety concerns. The officers, even if they speak limited English, are incredibly helpful and often have maps and resources to aid lost travelers.

Tourist Information Centers: Found in major stations like Tokyo and Shinjuku, these centers are staffed with English-speaking personnel ready to assist with travel inquiries, offer recommendations, and even help with bookings. They're invaluable resources for everything from navigating the city to finding cultural experiences.

Hospitals and Clinics: For medical concerns, Tokyo's larger hospitals often have English-speaking staff and international departments to assist foreign patients. Pharmacies also dot the city, with pharmacists who, despite the language barrier, are skilled at assisting through pictures and translation apps.

Embassies and Consulates: In more serious situations, your country's embassy or consulate can provide assistance with legal issues, lost passports, and emergencies. It's wise to keep their contact information handy.

Helplines and Apps: Tokyo offers various helplines for tourists, including English-speaking hotlines for medical, legal, and general assistance. Additionally, smartphone apps can connect you to emergency services, translation help, and even instant advice from locals.

Here are additional insights to ensure you're always within reach of assistance:

Disaster Preparedness Apps: Tokyo is ahead of the curve with apps specifically designed for disaster information, providing real-time alerts and safety tips for earthquakes, typhoons, or other emergencies.

Multilingual Support at ATMs: Many ATMs in convenience stores and banks offer multilingual support, ensuring you can securely access your funds without language barriers.

Wi-Fi Connectivity for Emergency Services: Tokyo's extensive public Wi-Fi network can be a lifeline for accessing help online, including emergency services and location-based assistance.

Community Support Groups: Tokyo has active expat and traveler communities online that offer advice, support, and assistance for navigating life and emergencies in the city, from healthcare questions to lost passport advice.

Medical Translation Services: Some services offer on-call translation for medical appointments or emergencies, bridging the communication gap and ensuring you receive the care you need without misunderstandings.

These additional layers of support within Tokyo's infrastructure not only keep you safe but also deepen your connection to the city, knowing that every adventure is backed by a robust network of assistance,

PREPARING FOR EARTHQUAKES

In Tokyo, the vibrancy of life is matched only by the city's preparedness for nature's unpredictability. Earthquakes, a part of life in Japan, are met with a calm and prepared response, a testament to the resilience ingrained in the city's fabric. As a traveler, stepping into Tokyo's rhythm means adopting a slice of this preparedness, blending awareness with the excitement of exploration.

Understanding that earthquakes can occur without warning is the first step. Tokyo's infrastructure and community are built to withstand and respond to these natural events, offering lessons in preparedness and resilience. Buildings, bridges, and public transport systems are engineered with earthquake resistance in mind, and emergency drills are a regular part of life, ensuring that the city's heartbeat continues uninterrupted, even in the face of nature's might.

Being earthquake-ready involves a few practical steps, seamlessly integrating into your adventure without casting a shadow over the joys of discovery. Knowing the basics of earthquake safety—such as the "Drop, Cover, and Hold On" method, familiarizing yourself with the emergency exits in your accommodation, and keeping a small emergency kit in your day pack —ensures you're not just a visitor but a prepared part of Tokyo's tapestry.

Staying informed while you're in Tokyo bridges the gap between awareness and action. Mobile apps dedicated to earthquake alerts, available in multiple languages, offer real-time information, allowing you to respond with informed calmness. These digital sentinels, coupled with the city's robust alert systems, ensure that you're never caught off guard, turning preparedness into an integrated aspect of your Tokyo experience.

Understanding the Early Warning System: Japan has an advanced Earthquake Early Warning (EEW) system that sends alerts through television, radio, and cell phones seconds before an earthquake hits. Familiarizing yourself with these alerts can give you precious seconds to react.

Locate the Nearest Evacuation Areas: Tokyo is equipped with designated evacuation areas in case of major disasters. Identifying the nearest evacuation site from your accommodation upon arrival can be a lifesaver.

Emergency Supplies in Vending Machines: In addition to regular snacks and drinks, some vending machines in Tokyo are equipped with emergency supplies like water, food, and blankets. Knowing how to spot these can be incredibly helpful in a pinch.

Communication Plan: In the event of a major earthquake, communication networks might be overwhelmed. Having a plan in place to contact your embassy, family, or friends after checking in at a safe location is essential.

Portable Wi-Fi or SIM Card: Keeping your phone connected allows you to receive real-time updates and use navigation apps to find evacuation routes or shelters.

Carry Identification and Key Information: Always have a copy of your passport, visa, and emergency contact information on you. This is crucial for identification or in case you need assistance from local authorities or your embassy.

Basic Japanese Phrases for Emergencies: Learning a few emergency-related Japanese phrases can help in situations where you need to seek help or understand instructions from locals.

Participate in Disaster Drills: If your visit coincides with a public disaster drill, consider participating or observing. These drills, often held in schools, community centers, or city wards, offer practical insights into the local approach to safety during earthquakes.

Stay Informed Through Local News: Keeping an eye on local news, even if it's just the English segments or newspapers, can offer additional context to any alerts you might receive and provide detailed instructions or advisories specific to your area.

Familiarize Yourself with Building Safety Features: Modern buildings in Tokyo are designed with earthquakes in mind. Knowing about safety features like earthquake-resistant structures, emergency exits, and evacuation chairs can add an extra layer of reassurance.

Know How to Use Fire Extinguishers and First-Aid Kits: Basic knowledge of how to use fire extinguishers and first-aid kits can be invaluable, not just for earthquakes but for any emergency. Many accommodations have these on-site, and a quick review of how to use them upon arrival is a good practice.

Emergency Contacts List: Beyond just having the list, ensure it's accessible even without internet access. A small, waterproof card with essential numbers and addresses can be a simple yet effective tool.

Mental Preparedness: While physical preparedness is crucial, mental readiness can't be overlooked. Familiarizing yourself with the potential scenarios and knowing your response plan can reduce panic and enable you to act more decisively if needed.

CHAPTER 2
GETTING AROUND TOKYO

2.1 USING PUBLIC TRANSPORT

TRAINS, SUBWAYS, AND MORE

Tokyo's trains and subways are not just modes of transport; they're the arteries that keep the city alive, buzzing from the crack of dawn till long after the stars are out.

The Train Network: Imagine a network so vast and efficient, it can whisk you from the historic temples of Asakusa to the futuristic vibes of Odaiba in no time. The trains in Tokyo, operated by various companies, form a grid that covers not just the city but extends its fingers into the neighboring prefectures. The JR Yamanote Line, a circular route connecting Tokyo's major city centers, is your golden circle of exploration, offering a window to the city's soul.

Subway Lines: Dive deeper, and the subway lines weave you through the city's underbelly, each color-coded route a path to new discoveries. Tokyo Metro and Toei Subway lines crisscross beneath the streets, their frequent stops punctuating every significant neighborhood, landmark, and hidden gem. Navigating the subway is a breeze with English signs and announcements, guiding you through the city's depths with confidence.

Beyond the Basics: But Tokyo's public transport doesn't end with trains and subways. Buses, though less frequented by tourists, offer routes that trains don't cover, reaching into the quieter, more intimate corners of Tokyo life. Then there's the monorail and automated guideways, providing scenic views of the bay and access to islands like Odaiba, adding a touch of adventure to your commute.

Navigating with Ease: Embrace technology to master this network. Apps that offer real-time schedules, route planning, and fare calculations turn what seems like a daunting web into a tailored path that leads exactly where you want to go. And with the Pasmo or Suica card, a tap is all it takes to access almost any mode of transport, simplifying your journey to a single swipe.

Cultural Nuances: Riding Tokyo's public transport is also a lesson in local etiquette. It's where silence is golden, priority seats are respected, and queues are meticulously formed. It's a space where the city's disciplined harmony shines, and participating in this unspoken dance connects you deeper to the fabric of Tokyo.

In Tokyo, moving from point A to B is more than just travel; it's an integral part of the city experience, a way to feel the city's heartbeat.

Late-Night Services: Most trains and subways in Tokyo wrap up before midnight, leading to a surge of taxis and rideshares. Knowing the last train times can save you from unexpected late-night expenses.

Women-Only Carriages: During rush hours, some trains offer women-only carriages to provide a safe and comfortable journey. These are clearly marked and typically available during the busiest times.

Bicycle Rentals: For short distances or exploring local neighborhoods, Tokyo's public bicycle sharing system offers an eco-friendly and health-conscious alternative to motorized public transport.

Festival Crowds: During major festivals or events, some train stations near the event sites might adjust their operations to manage the crowd better. Keeping an eye on these changes can enhance your festival experience.

Emergency Stop Buttons: Trains are equipped with emergency stop buttons, but they're meant for serious emergencies only. Accidentally pressing one can cause delays and might lead to fines.

THE MAGIC OF TRAVEL CARDS

Imagine holding a small, unassuming card, no bigger than a credit card, yet it holds the power to whisk you away to every corner of Tokyo, from the serene heights of Mt. Takao to the vibrant markets of Tsukiji. This is no ordinary card; this is your access to an adventure as fluid and dynamic as Tokyo itself.

PASMO and Suica: These two travel cards are more than just tickets; they're your companions on a journey through the heart of Tokyo. Both cards work interchangeably across almost all of Tokyo's public transport systems, including buses, trains, and even some taxis, making them indispensable tools for the urban explorer. The true beauty of these cards lies in their simplicity—load them with money at any ticket machine, and you're set to navigate the city with just a tap, avoiding the hassle of buying individual tickets or fumbling with change.

Beyond Transportation: But the magic of these cards extends beyond mere transit. They double as electronic wallets, granting you the power to make purchases at convenience stores, vending machines, and even some restaurants throughout the city. This seamless integration into Tokyo's daily life allows you to experience the city like a local, where buying a morning coffee or a quick snack is as simple as a tap of your card.

Special Edition Cards: For those looking for a unique memento from their Tokyo travels, special edition PASMO and Suica cards feature designs ranging from popular anime characters to seasonal landscapes of Japan. These limited-edition cards offer a tangible piece of the magic of Tokyo, a keepsake that carries the memories of your travels within its chip.

The Art of Recharging: Recharging these cards is a breeze, with machines available in every station, often with multilingual options. The act of topping up your card becomes a ritual, a moment of pause in your journey to reflect on where you've been and where you're headed next.

In the vast, intertwined network of Tokyo's public transport, PASMO and Suica cards emerge as more than mere conveniences; they are the embodiment of freedom. With one in your pocket, Tokyo opens up to you in all its diversity, ready to be explored without limits or boundaries.

These cards aren't just for tapping in and out of stations; they're embedded with features and possibilities that many travelers might not be aware of. For instance, both PASMO and Suica cards can be linked to digital payment systems like Apple Pay or Google Wallet, transforming your smartphone into a virtual travel card. This integration not only streamlines your travel but also adds a layer of security, as you can lock your phone if it gets lost or stolen, safeguarding your funds.

There are often seasonal or collaboration campaigns associated with these cards, offering discounts or special access to events, museums, and attractions across Tokyo. By keeping an eye on the official PASMO or Suica websites, you can tap into these deals, stretching your yen further and unlocking experiences you might not have discovered otherwise.

The refund process for any remaining balance on these cards is straightforward, ensuring that you can recoup your unused funds before leaving Japan. However, many travelers choose to keep their cards as souvenirs or for use on future trips, as the cards and their balances remain valid for several years.

RUSH HOUR SURVIVAL

Rush hour in Tokyo is a spectacle in itself, a testament to the city's pulsating energy and the disciplined flow of its inhabitants. As millions of people move in harmony, the uninitiated might find themselves overwhelmed. Yet, with a few strategies and insights, you can navigate this dense sea of commuters with the grace of a seasoned Tokyoite.

Timing is Everything: Tokyo's rush hours typically run from 7:30 to 9:30 in the morning and then again from 5:00 to 7:00 in the evening. These times see the city's trains and subways at their most crowded, with commuters heading to and from work. If possible, plan your travels outside these peak hours. Exploring Tokyo in the late morning or early afternoon offers a more relaxed journey, allowing you to enjoy the city's sights and sounds without the press of the crowd.

Choose Your Car Wisely: If you find yourself needing to travel during rush hour, knowing which train car to board can make all the difference. Some trains offer women-only cars during peak hours, providing a safe and less crowded space. Additionally, cars at the very front or back of the train tend to be slightly less crowded than those in the middle.

Pack Light and Tight: Navigating rush hour requires mobility and consideration for those around you. Pack essentials only and keep your belongings compact. Backpacks should be held in front of you or at your feet to make more room and prevent accidentally bumping into fellow passengers.

Embrace the Flow: There's an art to moving with the crowd in Tokyo, a rhythm to stepping on and off escalators, forming orderly lines, and boarding trains. Observing and mirroring the locals not only helps you blend in but also makes the rush hour dance feel less intimidating. It's about moving confidently, respecting personal space as much as possible, and following the unspoken rules that keep Tokyo moving smoothly.

Station Navigation: Larger stations can be as busy inside as the trains themselves during peak times. Familiarize yourself with the station layout in advance, noting exits and transfers to avoid last-minute confusion. Digital station maps and smartphone apps can be invaluable tools for planning your route through these transit hubs.

There are additional layers and tips that can further enhance your experience:

Exit Strategy: Knowing the correct exit at your destination station can save time and avoid the rush hour crowd. Tokyo stations often have numerous exits leading to different streets or landmarks.

Standing Position: During rush hours, position yourself near the train doors but out of the direct flow of boarding and alighting passengers. It makes for an easier exit and less jostling.

Alternative Routes: Sometimes taking a slightly longer route with fewer transfers or using less popular lines can result in a more comfortable journey, even if it takes a bit more time.

Off-Peak Travel Passes: Some travel cards offer discounts for traveling during off-peak hours, encouraging riders to avoid rush hour and save money.

Local Etiquette: If you find yourself in a packed train, it's customary to turn off or silence your phone and avoid talking loudly, creating a more pleasant environment for everyone.

2.2 SPEAKING IN TOKYO

HANDY JAPANESE PHRASES

Tokyo's melody is composed of more than just its bustling streets and whispering winds; it's in the greetings exchanged between friends, the gratitude shown to hosts, and the respectful nods between strangers. Mastering a handful of Japanese phrases is like learning the notes to this melody, allowing you to harmonize with the city's vibe, making each interaction a step closer to the heart of Tokyo.

Imagine walking into a quaint café tucked away in the winding streets of Shimokitazawa. As you step in, a simple "Konnichiwa" (Hello) breaks the ice, inviting smiles and a warm welcome. It's not just a greeting; it's an acknowledgment of the culture and respect that Tokyo holds dear.

Ordering your coffee, you might say "Kohi o kudasai" (Coffee, please). It's a simple phrase, but in a city that prides itself on service and hospitality, it's a gesture of politeness that's always appreciated. And when your order arrives, a heartfelt "Arigatou gozaimasu" (Thank you) not only expresses gratitude but also appreciation for the artistry and care put into your beverage.

But Tokyo's language of connection goes beyond the basics. Getting lost is a part of any great adventure in Tokyo, and asking for directions becomes a moment of human connection.

"Sumimasen, [location] wa doko desu ka?" (Excuse me, where is [location]?) opens up not just directions but often recommendations, insights, and sometimes, even personal stories.

Immersing yourself in its markets, temples, and bustling streets, a phrase like "Kore wa ikura desu ka?" (How much is this?) not only aids in your explorations but also invites interactions that are genuine and enriching, turning transactions into exchanges of culture.

Every phrase spoken in Japanese is more than just words; it's music to the ears of locals, an effort that's deeply appreciated and reciprocated with warmth and kindness. It transforms your journey from a mere visit into a series of meaningful encounters, each phrase a key unlocking deeper layers of the city's essence.

When the bustling city life sweeps you into its rapid stream, knowing how to express your curiosity and appreciation becomes invaluable. Venturing into a traditional Izakaya, you might find yourself enchanted by the array of dishes. Here, "Kore wa nan desu ka?" (What is this?) opens up a world of culinary exploration, inviting stories behind the dishes served, ingredients used, and the traditions they uphold.

In moments of sheer awe, when the beauty of Tokyo's juxtapositions strikes you—the ancient temples shadowed by towering skyscrapers, or the serene gardens encircled by the city's relentless energy—"Sugoi desu ne!" (That's amazing!) captures your wonder, sharing your admiration with those around you, and often, this shared appreciation leads to deeper conversations and insights into Tokyo's multifaceted identity.

Navigating Tokyo's vast expanse, you might also seek moments of tranquility, perhaps in one of its many parks or galleries. Here, "Shizuka na basho wa arimasu ka?" (Is there a quiet place?) not only guides you to oases of calm but also shows your respect for the culture's value of balance and harmony, inviting locals to share their personal escapes within the city.

As your day winds down, and the city lights begin to dance across the night sky, a simple "Oyasumi nasai" (Goodnight) to your hosts or new friends captures the gratitude and respect for the day's experiences and the hospitality received.

Here is a list of 20 phrases:

- **Konnichiwa** (こんにちは) - Hello.
- **Arigatou gozaimasu** (ありがとうございます) - Thank you very much.
- **Sumimasen** (すみません) - Excuse me/I'm sorry.
- **Eigo o hanasemasu ka?** (英語を話せますか?) - Do you speak English?
- **Toire wa doko desu ka?** (トイレはどこですか?) - Where is the bathroom?
- **Ikura desu ka?** (いくらですか?) - How much is it?
- **Kudasai** (ください) - Please.
- **Kore wa nan desu ka?** (これは何ですか?) - What is this?
- **Chizu o misete kudasai** (地図を見せてください) - Please show me the map.
- **Wi-Fi wa arimasu ka?** (Wi-Fiはありますか?) - Is there Wi-Fi?
- **Kippu uriba wa doko desu ka?** (切符売り場はどこですか?) - Where is the ticket office?
- **Densha wa nanji ni demasu ka?** (電車は何時に出ますか?) - What time does the train leave?
- **Mizu o kudasai** (水をください) - Water, please.
- **Mou ichido itte kudasai** (もう一度言ってください) - Please say it again.
- **Tetsudatte kudasai** (手伝ってください) - Please help me.
- **Yoyaku o shitai desu** (予約をしたいです) - I would like to make a reservation.
- **Kono chikaku ni osusume no restaurant wa arimasu ka?** (この近くにおすすめのレストランはありますか?) - Is there a recommended restaurant nearby?

- **Koko kara eki made arukimasu ka?** (ここから駅まで歩きますか?) - Is it walkable to the station from here?
- **Norikae wa arimasu ka?** (乗り換えはありますか?) - Are there any transfers?
- **Oyasumi nasai** (おやすみなさい) - Goodnight.

Beyond the basics, there are phrases that can transform your travel experience, making each moment more personal and memorable:

- Greeting shop staff with "Irasshaimase" (welcome) as you enter, showing appreciation for their hospitality.
- Using "Oishii desu" (this is delicious) at a restaurant to express your enjoyment of the meal directly to the chef or staff, which is always well-received.
- Saying "Gomen nasai" (I'm sorry) for any inconvenience you might cause, a phrase that goes a long way in showing respect for Japanese etiquette.
- Asking for recommendations with "Osusume wa nan desu ka?" (What do you recommend?) to engage locals and discover hidden gems.
- Ending your day with "Otsukaresama desu" (You're tired, thank you for your hard work) to express gratitude towards anyone who helped you, acknowledging their effort and care.
- These phrases peel back the layers of Tokyo's bustling exterior, revealing a culture of respect, appreciation, and community.

READING SIGNS AND MENUS

The city's language of symbols, a blend of the traditional Kanji characters with the more modern Hiragana and Katakana, paints a picture of a metropolis that's deeply rooted in its past yet always reaching for the future.

Navigating the City: Tokyo's signs, from street names to subway maps, often come with English translations, a nod to the city's welcoming embrace of travelers. Yet, the real magic lies in recognizing a few key characters. Knowing "出口" (exit) in Kanji can be a beacon in the intricate labyrinths of Tokyo's train stations, guiding you towards your next adventure. Similarly, "入口" (entrance) welcomes you into places unseen and stories untold, from the serene gardens hidden in the city's heart to the bustling markets that offer a feast for the senses.

The Culinary Expedition: Menus in Tokyo are a gateway to an unparalleled culinary journey. While picture menus and English translations are increasingly common, especially in tourist-friendly areas, the joy of decoding a menu written in Japanese is unparalleled. It's here that "定食" (set meal) promises a harmonious blend of flavors designed by the chef, and "刺身" (sashimi) invites you to taste the ocean's bounty, fresh and unadorned. Learning to recognize these characters opens up a world of flavors, where each dish is a discovery, and every meal is a voyage.

A Blend of Symbols: Tokyo's signage, a mix of pictograms and bilingual directions, ensures that even the uninitiated aren't lost for long. The universal symbols for restrooms, Wi-Fi, and smoking areas, coupled with Japanese characters, create a navigational dance that's both intriguing and accessible. The ubiquitous "Wi-Fi" symbol, often accompanied by "無料" (free), becomes a signpost for digital connectivity, ensuring you're never too far from the world beyond. In contrast, the stark "禁煙" (no smoking) or the inviting "喫煙所" (smoking area) signs navigate the city's health-conscious ethos, balancing the needs and comforts of all who wander its streets.

Embracing the Menu Adventure: Venturing further into the culinary landscape, the exploration becomes more nuanced. "季節の" (seasonal) whispers the secrets of dishes that change with the turning of the earth, offering flavors at their peak. Meanwhile, "限定" (limited) hints at exclusive creations, fleeting and unique, urging a taste before they vanish with the setting sun. This journey through the menu, guided by symbols and characters, is not just about sustenance but about experiencing Tokyo's heartbeat, one meal at a time.

The Art of Asking: Despite the aids of translations and symbols, there comes a moment in every traveler's journey where the path seems unclear. Here, the simple act of asking, "英語のメニューはありますか?" (Do you have an English menu?), becomes a key to unlock deeper understanding. It's an invitation for interaction, where language barriers dissolve over shared smiles and the universal love for good food.

In the heart of Tokyo, where signs and menus are the canvas, your willingness to read beyond the words—to see the history, culture, and innovation that they represent—transforms your journey. It's no longer about merely getting from point A to point B or from hunger to satisfaction. It's about weaving through the fabric of Tokyo, with each character and symbol a thread in the larger tapestry of this mesmerizing city.

As you become more attuned to the silent language of Tokyo, you start to notice the subtleties that give the city its character—the quaint sign of a centuries-old shop in Asakusa, the meticulously handwritten menu outside a hidden gem of a restaurant in Nakameguro, each telling stories of tradition, innovation, and passion.

The Cultural Connection: The act of reading in Tokyo goes beyond practicality—it's a bridge to the city's soul. The signs are not just indicators but invitations to experience the layers of history and modernity coexisting in harmony. A temple sign in ancient Kanji standing steadfast amidst the digital displays of Akihabara highlights Tokyo's ability to honor its past while racing towards the future.

A Taste of Authenticity: Menus become your guide to authentic Japanese cuisine, far removed from the familiar. They challenge you to venture beyond comfort zones, to try "natto" (fermented soybeans) or "umeboshi" (pickled plum), guided by curiosity and the thrill of new experiences. Each dish becomes a lesson in the diversity of Japanese cuisine, a story of regions, seasons, and the meticulous care put into food.

The Joy of Shared Experiences: Sharing these discoveries on social media, translating a sign for a fellow traveler, or recommending a dish you bravely decoded and thoroughly enjoyed adds layers of shared human experience to your journey. Tokyo, in its vastness, becomes a place of connections, made richer through the shared language of exploration and discovery.

Continuing the Learning Journey: As your familiarity with Tokyo's written language grows, so does your confidence to explore deeper, to take the path less traveled, to enter a shop with no English sign in sight, knowing that within lies a piece of Tokyo waiting to be discovered. This knowledge encourages not just exploration but also respect and appreciation for the culture and the people who make Tokyo the vibrant, pulsating metropolis it is.

Practical know-how that enriches your journey:

- Many restaurants display plastic or wax replicas of their dishes outside, offering a visual menu that helps you decide even before you walk in.
- QR codes are increasingly used on signs and menus, linking directly to websites or digital menus in multiple languages, making it easier to understand your options.
- Electronic ordering systems in restaurants, often with multilingual support, streamline the dining experience, allowing for customization of orders without the language barrier.

- Kanji for common allergens and dietary preferences can be a lifesaver for those with specific dietary needs, making it easier to navigate menus and communicate with restaurant staff.
- Learning the symbols for male (男) and female (女) bathrooms prevents any confusion in public spaces, ensuring a smoother experience as you explore the city.

These additional layers of understanding not only make navigating Tokyo's culinary and cultural landscape more accessible but also add an element of discovery and adventure to your travels, making every meal and every sign a part of your Tokyo story.

BREAKING THE LANGUAGE BARRIER

Tokyo, a city where silence speaks volumes and a bow can say more than a thousand words, presents a unique challenge and opportunity to its visitors. Breaking the language barrier here isn't merely about mastering a list of phrases but about engaging with the city and its people in a dance of non-verbal cues, technology, and the universal language of respect and curiosity.

Embrace Technology: In Tokyo's technologically advanced landscape, apps become your bridge over the language gap. Translation apps that convert text and speech in real time are like magic wands at your fingertips, turning daunting kanji into understandable sentences and unfamiliar signs into welcoming directions. Picture menus and digital ordering systems in restaurants invite you to explore Japanese cuisine without fear, each tap bringing you closer to the heart of Tokyo's food culture.

Non-Verbal Communication: The art of non-verbal communication in Tokyo opens up a new dimension of interaction. A respectful bow, a polite gesture indicating "no" with a gentle wave of your hand, and the attentive body language during conversations speak volumes. In the crowded trains, the silent exchange of glances that conveys understanding and the shared experience of the moment becomes a subtle form of connection.

Cultural Immersion Workshops: Engaging in cultural workshops offers a dual benefit: learning traditional arts, from calligraphy to tea ceremony, while naturally absorbing phrases and cultural nuances. These experiences do more than break the language barrier; they weave you into the very fabric of Tokyo's culture, making each learned word a treasure and each interaction a cherished memory.

Language Exchange Meetups: Tokyo thrives on exchange, and language meetups are a testament to this. Engaging with locals eager to practice English while you take a dive into conversational Japanese is not just about language learning; it's about building bridges, sharing stories, and understanding the city through the eyes of its inhabitants.

Patience and Humor: Navigating the language barrier often requires patience and a sense of humor. Misunderstandings can lead to laughter and memorable exchanges, turning what could be seen as a barrier into an opportunity for genuine, heartwarming connections.

Breaking the language barrier is an adventure in itself, a journey that takes you from the neon-lit streets of Shibuya to the tranquil gardens of the Imperial Palace, from the bustling markets of Tsukiji to the serene heights of Mount Takao. It's an exploration that goes beyond words, where every attempt to communicate opens a door to deeper understanding and every shared moment becomes a thread in the vibrant mosaic of your Tokyo experience.

Here are some additional strategies and insights that can enhance your experience:

Use Visual Aids: Carrying a small notebook or using your smartphone to show pictures or drawings can help convey your message when words fail. This is especially handy in restaurants or when looking for a specific place or item.

Learn Key Symbols: Familiarize yourself with common symbols used in public places, such as restrooms, exits, and prohibited items. These can help you navigate spaces more easily without needing to ask for directions constantly.

Download Offline Maps: Having access to maps that can be used without an internet connection ensures you're never truly lost, even if you can't communicate your destination verbally.

Gesture Carefully: Be mindful of your gestures, as some may have different meanings in Japan. Simple nods, smiles, and pointing (politely) are generally understood and accepted.

Seek Out Bilingual Locals: Younger Tokyo residents often have a basic understanding of English and are usually eager to practice. They can be invaluable resources for directions, recommendations, and insights into local culture.

Emergency Phrases: Knowing a few emergency phrases or having them written down can be crucial, such as asking for help or explaining a medical condition.

These approaches not only help in navigating the language barrier but also in enriching your travel experience, making every interaction an opportunity for learning and connection.

2.3 UNDERSTANDING TOKYO MANNERS

DO THIS, NOT THAT

Navigating Tokyo's societal norms is like learning a new language, one of respect, harmony, and mindfulness. It's not merely about avoiding missteps but about moving in sync with the city's rhythm, where every action reflects a deeper understanding and appreciation of its culture.

Do Bow, Don't Hug: In Tokyo, a bow ranges from a slight nod of the head to a deeper bend at the waist, a gesture of respect, gratitude, or apology. Unlike the warm hugs you might share back home, personal space is cherished here, and a bow perfectly bridges that distance with warmth and respect.

Do Queue, Don't Push: Whether waiting for the train, boarding a bus, or lining up at a popular eatery, orderly queues symbolize the city's collective respect for each other's space and time. Jumping the queue or pushing past others disrupts this harmony, a faux pas in Tokyo's unwritten manual of manners.

Do Silence Your Phone, Don't Talk Loudly on Public Transport: The calm that envelopes Tokyo's public transport is a sanctuary for many. Silencing your phone and keeping conversations to a whisper preserves this peace, allowing everyone a moment of respite in their busy lives.

Do Use Both Hands, Don't Point: When receiving or giving something, such as a business card or a gift, use both hands. It signifies the importance you place on the exchange. Conversely, pointing at people or objects is considered rude; instead, a gentle gesture with an open hand is preferred.

Do Enjoy Your Meal Quietly, Don't Tip: Slurping your noodles might be a sign of enjoyment, but general loud eating is frowned upon. And when the meal is done, resist the urge to tip. In Tokyo, exceptional service is a standard, not an extra to be compensated for with tips.

Do Take Off Your Shoes, Don't Ignore Tatami Etiquette: In many traditional settings, such as ryokans (Japanese inns), temples, and some restaurants, you'll be expected to remove your shoes. Stepping onto tatami mats with shoes or even slippers can be seen as disrespecting the space.

Do Carry Your Trash, Don't Litter: Tokyo's streets are remarkably clean, not because of an abundance of public trash cans, but because locals take their trash with them until they find the appropriate place to dispose of it. Following suit not only shows respect for the city but also for the environment.

Manners are more than just a set of rules; they're a reflection of the city's soul, a way to connect with its history, people, and ethos. As you step in time with Tokyo's rhythm, each mindful action and respectful gesture weaves you deeper into the fabric of the city, transforming you from an observer to an active participant in its daily life.

There are nuanced practices that enhance the cultural experience:

Handling Chopsticks: Never stick them upright in a bowl of rice, as this resembles a funeral rite. Instead, rest them on a chopstick holder or the edge of your plate when not in use.

Respecting Privacy: Avoid taking photos of people without their permission, especially in sacred or private spaces like temples, shrines, or private gardens.

Quiet Spaces: Many public places, such as libraries, museums, and certain gardens, are considered quiet zones. Keeping your voice down in these areas is appreciated.

Recycling: Tokyo takes recycling seriously. Pay attention to the separation of recyclables and non-recyclables when disposing of waste.

Escalator Etiquette: Stand on one side (usually the left in Tokyo, but it can vary by city) to let others pass on the opposite side.

Seasonal Greetings: Use "Otsukaresama desu" (You're tired) at the end of the day or work-related activities and "Kyou mo atsukaresama desu" (Thank you for your hard work today) for a more personalized touch.

HOW TO EAT WITHOUT OOPS

Dining scene is a mosaic of flavors, textures, and colors, each dish telling a story of history, season, and craftsmanship. To partake in this culinary narrative without a faux pas requires not just an appetite but an understanding of the dining etiquette that adorns Tokyo's tables.

As you slide open the door to a traditional izakaya or settle into the serene setting of a sushi counter, the first whisper of etiquette greets you with an oshibori, a warm, damp towel. This is not merely for cleaning your hands but a ritual to prepare you for the meal ahead, a moment to transition from the bustling streets to the culinary journey you're about to embark on.

With chopsticks in hand, the ballet of dining etiquette unfolds. These are not mere utensils but extensions of your intentions, to be used with precision and respect. Remember, passing food directly from one set of chopsticks to another mirrors a funeral rite and is to be avoided. Instead, if sharing, place the item on a shared plate for another to pick up. And when pausing, rest your chopsticks on a holder or the edge of your bowl, never sticking them upright, a gesture that evokes offerings to the departed.

The act of eating in Tokyo is as much about appreciation as it is about nourishment. When served a dish, take a moment to admire its presentation, the harmony of its colors, and the balance of its flavors. It's customary to express gratitude for the meal with a soft "itadakimasu" (I humbly receive) before beginning and a heartfelt "gochisosama deshita" (thank you for the feast) at its conclusion, acknowledging the chef's effort and the food's origin.

Slurping noodles is not just acceptable but appreciated, a sign of enjoying the meal. However, this auditory delight is reserved for noodles alone; other dishes prefer a quieter engagement. And while it's tempting to dive into the depths of a delicious bowl, lifting small portions of food to your mouth, rather than bringing your face to the bowl, maintains the elegance of the dining experience.

Sushi, a jewel in Tokyo's culinary crown, invites its own set of manners. It's a cuisine of simplicity and subtlety, where each piece is savored for its individual flavor and texture. Use chopsticks or, in some cases, your hands, and dip the fish side lightly into soy sauce, avoiding soaking the rice, which respects the chef's balance of flavors.

Here are additional insights to ensure a smooth culinary experience:

Seasonal Sensitivity: Tokyo's chefs pride themselves on using seasonal ingredients. Showing appreciation or asking about the season's specialties can enhance your dining experience and demonstrate respect for the chef's expertise.

Sake Etiquette: When drinking sake in a group, it's customary to serve each other rather than pouring for oneself. This practice fosters a sense of companionship and mutual respect.

Handling Condiments: Be mindful with condiments like soy sauce and wasabi. Adding too much can imply dissatisfaction with the chef's preparation, as dishes are often served with the intended balance of flavors.

Payment Practices: In many traditional eateries, the bill is not brought to the table but is settled at a designated counter near the entrance. Look for the sign "会計" (kaikei) pointing to where you pay.

These practices not only smooth the path to enjoying Tokyo's culinary scene but also deepen your appreciation for the city's rich gastronomic culture, making each meal a memorable part of your Tokyo adventure.

TEMPLE AND SHRINE DOS

These spaces, rich with history and spirituality, demand a certain reverence, a mindfulness of actions and attitudes that honor their sanctity.

Approach with Respect: The transition from the bustling city streets to the hallowed grounds of a temple or shrine begins with a bow. It's a gesture of respect, acknowledging the sacredness of the space you're about to enter. This silent greeting sets the tone for your visit, marking a shift from the secular to the spiritual.

Purification Rites: Near the entrance, you'll often find a chozuya, a water pavilion for ritual cleansing. Using a ladle, pour water over your left hand, then your right, cleanse your mouth (without drinking directly from the ladle), and finally, rinse your left hand again. This act of purification, both physical and symbolic, prepares you to engage with the divine.

Offering and Prayer: Making an offering at a shrine, typically a few coins tossed into an offering box, is followed by a short prayer or moment of silence. The act isn't about the monetary value but the intention behind it—a gesture of respect and humility. Follow the local custom: bow twice, clap twice, and bow once more after your prayer, a rhythm that echoes the heartbeat of Tokyo's spiritual life.

Photography with Sensitivity: While many temples and shrines welcome photography, capturing the beauty of these spaces, certain areas may prohibit it, especially interior spaces where deities reside. Look for signs or ask for permission if unsure. Photographs should capture the essence of the place without intruding on the privacy of others engaged in prayer or meditation.

Silence is Golden: The serene atmosphere of temples and shrines is a sanctuary for many seeking solace from the city's clamor. Conversations should be kept to whispers, if necessary, allowing everyone the space to reflect, pray, and find peace.

Mindful Exploration: Many temples and shrines are home to gardens, museums, and historical artifacts, each telling a part of Tokyo's rich tapestry of history and belief. Exploring these spaces with mindfulness and curiosity not only enriches your understanding but also deepens your connection to Tokyo's cultural and spiritual dimensions.

Visiting temples and shrines in Tokyo is a pilgrimage into the heart of Japan's cultural and spiritual identity. Each step taken with respect, each gesture made with mindfulness, bridges the gap between visitor and local, between the present and the past.

Here are more insights to enhance your visit:

Seasonal Events: Many temples and shrines host seasonal festivals or special events. Participating or observing these can offer a deeper understanding of Japanese culture and traditions.

Ema Boards: You can write wishes or prayers on wooden plaques called "ema" and hang them at the shrine. It's a beautiful way to leave a part of yourself behind in a respectful manner.

Omikuji: Try your luck with omikuji, fortune-telling strips found at shrines. It's a fun way to engage with tradition, and if you get a bad fortune, you can tie it onto a designated rack to leave the bad luck behind.

No Eating or Drinking: While walking through the sacred grounds, refrain from eating or drinking. It's about maintaining the purity and serenity of the space.

Respect Closed Areas: Some areas within temples and shrines may be off-limits to visitors. Respecting these boundaries is crucial, as they often hold significant religious importance.

2.4 WHERE TO SLEEP

PICKING YOUR PERFECT STAY

Tokyo, a city of endless contrasts and possibilities, offers a kaleidoscope of accommodations, each with its unique charm and appeal. Whether you're seeking the pulsating heart of the city's nightlife, the serene embrace of a traditional inn, or the cutting-edge comfort of a luxury hotel, Tokyo invites you to dream in every shade.

Immerse in Tradition at a Ryokan: For those seeking a taste of traditional Japan, a stay at a ryokan offers more than just a bed for the night. It's a cultural experience, where tatami floors, futon beds, and sliding shoji doors transport you to a world where every detail speaks of care and tradition. Here, hospitality is an art form, and every meal is a feast for the senses, making each moment of your stay a step deeper into Japanese culture.

Embrace Modernity in City Hotels: If the pulse of the city calls to you, Tokyo's modern hotels stand as beacons of comfort and convenience amidst the urban energy. From towering skyscrapers offering panoramic views of the city's neon dance to boutique hotels where modern art and design meet, these stays are your gateway to Tokyo's vibrant heart, with the city's wonders just an elevator ride away.

Discover Unique Charm in Hostels: For the social traveler, Tokyo's hostels offer a unique blend of affordability, community, and creativity. More than just a place to sleep, these spaces are hubs of interaction, where travelers from around the world meet, share stories, and forge friendships. With communal spaces designed to inspire and connect, each hostel in Tokyo tells its own story, inviting you to be part of its narrative.

Find Solitude in Traditional Guesthouses: Nestled in quiet neighborhoods, traditional guesthouses, or "minshuku," offer a cozy, intimate look at Tokyo life. These family-run accommodations provide a home away from home, where simplicity and warmth pave the way to meaningful connections with the city and its people.

Luxury and Innovation in High-End Accommodations: For those seeking the ultimate in luxury and technology, Tokyo's high-end accommodations are unrivaled. Here, traditional

Japanese hospitality meets futuristic comfort, with rooms controlled by the touch of a tablet and services that cater to your every whim, all wrapped in the exquisite elegance of Japanese design.

Where every corner offers a new discovery, your choice of accommodation becomes part of the journey, a reflection of your personal adventure through this multifaceted city. Whether you're falling asleep to the quiet hum of a traditional garden or waking up to the electric buzz of the city, "Picking Your Perfect Stay" is about finding the space that speaks to you, inviting you to dream, explore, and immerse in the endless stories of this captivating city.

Accommodation scene reveals even more unique options and tips that can enhance your stay:

Capsule Hotels: Perfect for solo travelers looking for a unique and budget-friendly option. Each guest stays in a small, pod-like space which is surprisingly comfortable and efficient.

Love Hotels: Offering privacy and novelty, these hotels are designed for couples and are known for their themed rooms. They can be a fun, quirky choice for a night.

Business Hotels: Catering to travelers who prioritize convenience and functionality, business hotels in Tokyo offer compact, well-equipped rooms at reasonable prices, often located near train stations.

Vacation Rentals: For a more local experience or for those traveling in groups, renting an apartment or a house can be cost-effective and offer a glimpse into Tokyo life.

Stay near a Yamanote Line Station: Choosing accommodations near the Yamanote Line, Tokyo's main train loop, provides easy access to most major attractions and simplifies travel around the city.

HOW TO BOOK SMART

The key to finding your way lies not in the swift decision but in the art of booking smart, a blend of timing, research, and understanding Tokyo's unique rhythms.

Start Early, Stay Flexible: Tokyo's popularity means accommodations can fill up quickly, especially during cherry blossom season or major festivals. Starting your search early gives you a broader selection and often better prices. Yet, within this early planning, flexibility is your ally. Being open to different neighborhoods or types of accommodations can lead to discoveries that enrich your stay, turning a simple booking into the first chapter of your Tokyo story.

Leverage Technology: In a city that's at the forefront of the future, technology is your guide to booking smart. Use a mix of global and local booking platforms to explore a wide range of options, from international hotel chains to local guesthouses. Apps and websites specific to Japan can uncover hidden gems that global platforms might not list, offering you a more authentic stay.

Understand the Location: Tokyo's vast expanse means location is crucial. Staying near a major train line or within walking distance of a JR Yamanote Line station can save you time and simplify your daily explorations. Research the neighborhoods to find one that resonates with your travel style, whether it's the electric energy of Shibuya, the traditional charm of Asakusa, or the chic streets of Ginza.

Read Reviews, Seek Recommendations: In a city where every corner holds a story, reviews, and recommendations are your map to finding accommodations that align with your expectations. Look beyond the star rating to understand the experiences of fellow travelers. Blogs, forums, and social media can also offer insights and tips that guide your choice, connecting you with personal stories of Tokyo stays.

Consider the Amenities: Tokyo's accommodations are as varied in amenities as they are in style. From the communal baths of traditional ryokans to the high-tech comforts of luxury hotels, understanding what each place offers helps tailor your stay to your needs. Consider what's important to you—Wi-Fi, proximity to public transport, non-smoking rooms—and let these guide your booking.

Booking Direct vs. Third-Party Sites: While third-party sites might offer deals, booking directly through the hotel or guesthouse's website can sometimes unveil special rates or packages not available elsewhere. Direct booking also often allows for easier communication with the host, setting the stage for a warm welcome upon your arrival.

Where each day is a canvas of experiences, where to sleep is not just a practicality but a part of the adventure. Booking smart opens the door to stays that are more than just places to rest but are homes away from home, sanctuaries where each morning's awakening is the beginning of a new tale.

Accommodation booking experience, consider these additional tips:

Seasonal Rates: Be aware of how seasons affect pricing. Cherry blossom season and New Year can see a spike in costs and demand, while other times may offer more value.

Check-In/Out Times: Tokyo hotels often have strict check-in and check-out times. Knowing these can help plan your arrival and departure more smoothly.

Cancellation Policies: Especially when booking in advance, it's smart to understand the cancellation policies in case your plans change.

Local Accommodation Types: Beyond hotels and hostels, consider "manga cafes" for an overnight stay with internet access, or "love hotels" for their unique themes and privacy, even if just for the novelty.

Pocket Wi-Fi Rental: Some accommodations offer pocket Wi-Fi devices, which can be a huge bonus for staying connected while exploring the city.

Cultural Considerations: If staying in a ryokan or similar traditional lodging, familiarize yourself with etiquette such as removing shoes indoors and using communal baths appropriately.

BEST AREAS TO STAY IN

Navigating this diversity, you'll find areas that resonate with your travel style, whether you're seeking the electric buzz of the city, the whisper of tradition, or a blend of both.

Shibuya and Shinjuku: The heartbeats of Tokyo's ceaseless energy, these areas are where the city's iconic image comes to life. Skyscrapers, bustling streets, endless dining and shopping options, and some of the city's most famous landmarks make Shibuya and Shinjuku ideal for those who want to dive headfirst into Tokyo's modern pulse. Here, the night is as alive as the day, offering a glimpse into the city that never sleeps.

Asakusa: For a touch of the traditional, Asakusa's historic streets, framed by the majestic Senso-ji Temple and the vibrant Nakamise shopping street, offer a journey back in time. Staying in this area not only places you within walking distance of rich cultural sites but also offers a quieter, more reflective side of Tokyo, where the past is lovingly preserved amidst the rush of the present.

Ginza: The epitome of luxury, Ginza's polished streets are lined with high-end shops, galleries, and theaters, making it a haven for those seeking sophistication and style. Here, modernity meets elegance, and accommodations often provide a level of service and comfort that mirrors the district's luxurious ethos.

Roppongi: Known for its vibrant nightlife and art scene, Roppongi is a cultural hub that attracts a cosmopolitan crowd. With its mix of nightclubs, art museums, and international dining, staying in Roppongi offers a blend of cultural exploration and entertainment, perfect for the traveler looking to experience Tokyo's diverse global influences.

Ueno: For the nature and museum enthusiast, Ueno's sprawling park houses not just beautiful cherry blossoms but also some of Tokyo's most prestigious museums and a zoo. This area offers a peaceful retreat from the city's hustle, where culture, nature, and history intertwine, providing a serene backdrop for your Tokyo adventure.

Whether you're falling asleep to the view of neon lights, the quiet hum of a traditional alley, or the serene silence of a park, choosing the best area to stay in is about aligning your accommodation with the chapters you want to write in your Tokyo journey. So, let your heart guide you to the neighborhood that calls to you, knowing that in Tokyo, every area opens up a world of discovery, inviting you to not just visit but to belong.

Accommodation landscape further, here are additional insights into choosing the best area to stay:

Odaiba: Ideal for families or those seeking a futuristic vibe, with its entertainment complexes, shopping malls, and stunning views of the Rainbow Bridge.

Ebisu/Daikanyama: For a more laid-back atmosphere with stylish cafes, boutiques, and a more local feel, these neighboring areas offer a chic retreat from the city's frenzy.

Ikebukuro: A paradise for anime and manga fans, Ikebukuro is vibrant and packed with entertainment options, making it a lively base for pop culture enthusiasts.

Kichijoji: Nestled around the serene Inokashira Park, Kichijoji is filled with charming streets, vintage stores, and a relaxed vibe, perfect for those looking to experience Tokyo's hipster side.

Akihabara: The go-to area for tech-lovers and gamers, Akihabara's electric town offers a deep dive into Japan's otaku culture.

2.5 EXPLORING AREAS

BRIGHT LIGHTS: SHIBUYA AND SHINJUKU

Shibuya and Shinjuku, each a microcosm of Tokyo's boundless vitality, offer more than just a glimpse into urban life; they are the very essence of the city's dynamism. These areas, alive with light, sound, and ceaseless motion, beckon with promises of unforgettable experiences, each corner a new discovery, each moment a memory in the making.

Shibuya: The heartbeat of youth culture and fashion, Shibuya pulses with a rhythm all its own. The iconic Shibuya Crossing, a kaleidoscope of people weaving through the neon glow, offers the quintessential Tokyo moment. It's here among the towering screens and bustling cafes that trends are born and the city's pulse is felt most keenly. Beyond the crossing, Shibuya's streets unfold with hidden izakayas, boutique shops, and the tranquil Meiji Shrine, offering respite from the whirlwind of the streets.

Shinjuku: A district of contrasts, where the sleek skyscrapers of the government buildings meet the narrow alleys of Golden Gai, Shinjuku is Tokyo in microcosm. The area's west side is a testament to modernity, home to the Tokyo Metropolitan Government Building, whose observation decks offer sprawling views of the city. To the east, Shinjuku's entertainment district comes alive at night, with Kabukicho offering an array of dining, shopping, and entertainment options. The tranquil Shinjuku Gyoen National Garden provides a lush escape from the urban excitement, its sprawling lawns and quiet ponds a reminder of Tokyo's many faces.

Navigating the Bright Lights: Both Shibuya and Shinjuku are more than just destinations; they are experiences. Navigating these areas is to ride Tokyo's wave of ceaseless innovation and enduring tradition. The best approach is one of openness, allowing the city to guide your steps. Whether marveling at the Hachiko statue in Shibuya, a symbol of loyalty and a popular meeting spot, or exploring the warren-like bars of Golden Gai in Shinjuku, where each tiny establishment has its own unique character, the journey through these districts is one of discovery.

Embracing the Night: As day turns to night, Shibuya and Shinjuku transform. The neon lights shine brighter, the streets fill with the energy of night revelers, and the districts reveal their true character. This is when the true vibrancy of Tokyo comes to life, in the laughter spilling from izakayas, the buzz of the arcades, and the quiet moments of connection found in the city's nocturnal heart.

Shibuya's Diverse Lanes: Beyond the famed crossing, Shibuya's narrow lanes like Center Gai and Spain Slope are brimming with fashion boutiques, quirky shops, and vintage stores, each telling a story of Tokyo's youth culture. Venturing further, you'll encounter Yoyogi Park, an expansive green oasis where street performers, picnickers, and musicians gather, showcasing the city's creative pulse against a backdrop of tranquility.

Shinjuku's Hidden Worlds: Shinjuku's allure lies in its ability to hide worlds within worlds. Omoide Yokocho and Golden Gai, with their Showa-era charm, offer intimate glimpses into Tokyo's past through tiny bars and eateries that seat only a handful of guests. Each establishment has a story, with proprietors often sharing tales that paint a vivid picture of the district's rich history.

Culinary Adventures: Both districts serve as culinary heavens for food enthusiasts. Shibuya's Omotesando and Harajuku areas are not just about fashion; they're also home to trendy cafes and high-end restaurants where traditional Japanese cuisine meets global gastronomy. Meanwhile, Shinjuku, with its endless array of dining options, from street food stalls in Kabukicho to Michelin-starred restaurants, invites you to taste the world in a single district.

Cultural Immersion: Shibuya's cultural landscape is marked by landmarks like the Bunkamura, a cultural complex offering a mix of theater, cinema, and art exhibitions, reflecting the district's modern artistic sensibilities. Shinjuku, with its mix of art houses like the New National Theatre and the avant-garde performances in small, underground venues, showcases the depth of Tokyo's cultural scene.

Nightlife and Entertainment: When the sun sets, Shibuya and Shinjuku illuminate Tokyo's nightlife. Shibuya's clubs and bars pulse with the latest beats, attracting a young crowd ready to dance the night away. Shinjuku's Kabukicho, Japan's largest red-light district, transforms into a neon spectacle, with karaoke bars, clubs, and themed restaurants offering a night of escapades. Yet, amidst the revelry, places like Shinjuku Ni-chome, Tokyo's LGBTQ+ district, provide safe spaces for inclusive celebration and connection.

Navigating with Respect: As you explore these districts, remember the importance of navigating with respect for the local culture and community. Be mindful of residents' privacy, especially in more traditional or residential areas, and always seek permission before photographing people or private establishments.

Here are additional insights to enrich your Tokyo adventure:

Interactive Experiences: Both districts offer unique, interactive experiences like VR arcades and animal cafes, where you can enjoy a coffee surrounded by cats, rabbits, or even owls, adding a quirky touch to your visit.

Art and Design: Shibuya and Shinjuku are hotspots for street art and design, with galleries and pop-up exhibits showcasing local and international artists. Exploring these can offer a deeper understanding of Tokyo's artistic pulse.

Green Spaces: Apart from Yoyogi Park, both areas are close to hidden gardens and smaller parks, providing quiet retreats from the urban energy. Shinjuku Gyoen is particularly beautiful during cherry blossom season.

Market Shopping: While known for their nightlife and entertainment, both districts also host markets where you can find everything from vintage clothing to artisan crafts, offering a glimpse into Tokyo's diverse shopping culture.

Local Festivals: Depending on the time of your visit, you might catch local festivals or "matsuri" held in these areas, offering an immersive experience into Japanese traditions, complete with parades, traditional food, and performances.

OLD TOKYO: ASAKUSA AND UENO

Asakusa, with its narrow lanes and the iconic Kaminarimon Gate leading to Senso-ji Temple, is Tokyo's beating heart of tradition. Here, the air carries the scent of incense and the sounds of wooden prayer blocks clapping together, creating a rhythm that guides you through a marketplace of history. The shops lining Nakamise Street offer everything from handcrafted souvenirs to traditional sweets, each telling a story of Tokyo's rich cultural tapestry.

As you wander, the majestic sight of Senso-ji Temple unfolds, a symbol of resilience and faith. The temple, with its towering pagoda and vibrant lanterns, invites you to pause and reflect, offering a moment of tranquility amid the city's hustle. Nearby, the Asakusa Shrine stands as a testament to the enduring bond between the past and present, hosting festivals that light up the district with color and joy.

Ueno, a short journey away, presents a different facet of Old Tokyo. Ueno Park, a sprawling oasis of green, is home to lotus ponds, ancient statues, and cherry blossom trees that explode into a spectacle of pink in spring. The park is more than just a haven of nature; it's a cultural hub, surrounded by museums like the Tokyo National Museum and the Ueno Royal Museum, each doorway leading into a world of art, history, and science waiting to be discovered.

But Ueno's charm isn't confined to its park. The district's lanes are dotted with traditional restaurants and izakayas, where you can savor dishes that have nourished Tokyoites for generations. The Ameya-Yokocho market, a bustling alley of stalls selling everything from fresh seafood to clothing, offers a glimpse into Tokyo's post-war recovery, a place where the city's indomitable spirit shines.

Asakusa and Ueno are not just locations on a map; they are living museums, vibrant galleries of life where every street, every building, and every garden tells a story. To explore these districts is to walk through chapters of Tokyo's history, where ancient festivals, traditional crafts, and the serene beauty of nature coexist with the city's forward-looking dynamism.

Discovering the Hidden Alleys: Venturing into the backstreets of Asakusa reveals quaint tea houses and artisan workshops where time-honored crafts like indigo dyeing and fan making are kept alive by dedicated artisans. These quiet lanes, away from the main thoroughfares, are where you can witness the meticulous care and skill that define Tokyo's craftsmanship, offering a personal connection to the city's cultural heritage.

Cultural Workshops and Experiences: Both Asakusa and Ueno are hubs for cultural workshops that invite hands-on participation. From trying your hand at calligraphy in a serene studio to participating in a traditional tea ceremony, these experiences provide a deeper dive into Japanese customs and the Zen philosophy that permeates Tokyo's way of life. It's an opportunity to not just observe but to actively engage with the practices that have shaped Tokyo's identity.

Seasonal Events and Celebrations: The changing seasons bring a calendar of events and celebrations to Asakusa and Ueno, each adding a layer of festivity to the districts. In Asakusa, the Sanja Matsuri, one of Tokyo's largest and most vibrant festivals, fills the streets with music, dance, and portable shrines in a spirited display of community and tradition. Ueno's cherry blossom season transforms Ueno Park into a canvas of delicate pink, drawing locals and visitors alike into a centuries-old tradition of hanami (flower viewing), reflecting on the ephemeral beauty of life.

The Culinary Journey: Exploring Old Tokyo is also a journey through Japan's culinary landscape. Asakusa's streets are dotted with stalls selling traditional snacks like ningyo-yaki (small cakes filled with sweet red bean paste) and age-manju (deep-fried buns with various fillings), offering a taste of Tokyo's sweet side. Ueno's market areas serve up fresh, local ingredients in dishes that have sustained generations, from savory street food to elegant kaiseki meals, each bite a testament to Tokyo's gastronomic diversity.

Connecting with Nature: Both districts, despite their historical weight, offer green spaces that provide a peaceful escape from the urban rush. Ueno Park, with its Shinobazu Pond, is a haven for wildlife, particularly waterfowl, creating a serene environment where nature and culture meet. Similarly, Asakusa's Sumida River provides a picturesque backdrop for leisurely walks and boat tours, offering panoramic views of Tokyo's skyline juxtaposed against the tranquil waters.

Asakusa and Ueno, here are more unique insights:

Sumida River Fireworks: An annual spectacle that lights up the sky over Asakusa, offering a blend of tradition and celebration, perfect for experiencing Japan's love for fireworks.

Panda Watching: Ueno Zoo, Japan's oldest zoo, is famous for its pandas. Visiting early in the morning can beat the crowds for a calm viewing experience.

Retro Gaming: Akihabara is nearby, but Asakusa has its own spots for retro gaming and anime goods, offering a quieter alternative to explore otaku culture.

Asakusa's Traditional Hostels: Some hostels in Asakusa offer a mix of modern comfort with traditional aesthetics, perfect for budget travelers seeking a touch of Japanese style.

Ueno's Ameyoko Market: Beyond the usual, diving into side alleys reveals specialty shops selling everything from traditional Japanese instruments to military surplus.

Historical Museums: The Edo-Tokyo Museum near Ueno offers deep dives into Tokyo's past, with life-sized replicas and interactive exhibits.

These bits of information add layers to your Asakusa and Ueno visit, making your exploration richer and more connected.

COOL AND QUIRKY: AKIHABARA AND HARAJUKU

Akihabara, affectionately known as "Electric Town," is the epicenter of Japan's otaku culture. This district lights up with neon signs, towering anime billboards, and the buzz of electronics shops that stretch as far as the eye can see. Here, the future collides with fantasy, creating a playground for gamers, tech enthusiasts, and anime fans.

Walking through Akihabara, you're invited to dive into a world of maid cafes, where the concept of hospitality takes on a unique, thematic twist. Venture further, and you'll discover stores dedicated entirely to manga, retro video games, and electronic gadgets, each aisle offering a glimpse into Japan's cutting-edge creativity and its dedication to preserving every niche of pop culture.

Harajuku, on the other hand, serves as the canvas for Tokyo's fashion-forward youth. Takeshita Street, a narrow alley bursting with color, is where trends are born and individuality shines brightest. From vintage shops to high-end boutiques, Harajuku embraces all forms of self-expression, making it a must-visit for anyone looking to experience Tokyo's dynamic street fashion scene.

Beyond the bustling streets, Harajuku hides serene spaces like Meiji Shrine, offering a peaceful retreat amidst the excitement. This juxtaposition of the vibrant and the tranquil encapsulates the essence of Tokyo, a city of harmonious contrasts.

Navigating Akihabara and Harajuku requires more than just a map; it demands curiosity and an open mind. Engage with the districts' unique experiences, from trying your luck in a gachapon hall filled with capsule toys to savoring a crepe in Harajuku's fashion streets. Each corner reveals a new layer of Tokyo's culture, inviting you to partake in its ongoing story.

Cultural Immersion: Both districts offer more than just shopping and dining; they are living galleries of contemporary Japanese culture. Participating in a workshop to create your own kawaii (cute) accessories in Harajuku or joining a gaming tournament in an Akihabara arcade can offer deeper insights into the passions that drive Tokyo's youth.

Seasonal Events: Keep an eye out for seasonal events like Akihabara's electronics sales or Harajuku's fashion week, where the districts showcase their best and brightest, offering unique opportunities to engage with locals and visitors alike.

These districts, with their blend of the cool and quirky, invite you to explore, engage, and express, embodying the essence of a city that never stops dreaming.

Akihabara and Harajuku's unique vibe:

Themed Cafes Beyond Maids: Akihabara offers a variety of themed cafes, from animal cafes where you can relax with cats, bunnies, or even owls, to concept cafes based on popular video games and anime series, offering immersive experiences.

Street Performers in Harajuku: On weekends, Yoyogi Park, close to Harajuku, becomes a stage for street performers, musicians, and dance groups. It's a great spot to see Tokyo's artistic side in the open air.

DIY Fashion Workshops: Harajuku is not just about buying fashion; it's also about creating it. Several shops and studios offer workshops where you can make your own accessories or customize clothing, diving hands-on into the district's creative culture.

Akihabara's Gadget Shopping: Beyond mainstream electronics, Akihabara is a treasure trove for niche gadgets and DIY electronics kits. It's a haven for tech enthusiasts looking to explore robotics, build their own computers, or find rare parts.

Cosplay Shops: Both districts are great for cosplay enthusiasts. Akihabara focuses more on anime and manga characters, while Harajuku offers a broader range of costume shops catering to its unique fashion scene.

WAIT A MOMENT

We Hope You're Enjoying Your Adventure!

As you pause here, halfway through your journey with us, we hope you've found this guide to be a valuable companion on your travels. Your experiences and insights are incredibly important to us—and to fellow travelers too!

If you're enjoying our travel book, would you consider taking a moment to share your thoughts on Amazon? Your review not only helps us to improve but also guides other explorers in choosing their next adventure. It's simple, quick, and can make a huge difference.

Here's how to do it:

- **Visit the Book's Amazon Page**: Search for the book title on Amazon.
- **Leave a Review**: Click on the 'Customer Reviews' section and then select 'Write a Customer Review'.
- **Share Your Thoughts**: Tell others what you love about the book, how it's helped in your travels, and why you'd recommend it.

Every word you share helps us to create better guides and enriches the travel community. We can't wait to read about your journey and experiences. Thank you for being a part of our adventure!

Happy Travels,

Kaiyo Takum

CHAPTER 3
TOKYO'S MUST-VISITS

3.1 ICONIC SPOTS

SKYTREE VS. TOKYO TOWER

Tokyo Skytree: Rising majestically in the Sumida district, the Tokyo Skytree stands as a testament to modern engineering and design. At 634 meters, it is not just Japan's tallest structure but a beacon of innovation, reflecting the city's forward-looking spirit. The Skytree serves dual purposes: a television and radio broadcast site and a vantage point offering breathtaking views of Tokyo and beyond.

Visiting the Skytree transports you into a futuristic experience, starting with its sleek, spiraling design inspired by traditional Japanese aesthetics. Two observation decks, located at 350 and 450 meters, offer panoramic vistas that stretch to the horizon, providing a new perspective on Tokyo's vastness. The tower is also home to a shopping complex, Solamachi, offering a variety of shops, restaurants, and even an aquarium, making it a comprehensive entertainment destination.

Tokyo Tower: With its Eiffel Tower-inspired lattice design, the Tokyo Tower painted in white and international orange to comply with air safety regulations, stands as a beloved symbol of post-war Japan's rebirth and growth. At 333 meters, it offers a nostalgic charm and a reminder of Tokyo's resilience and enduring beauty.

The Tokyo Tower's main observatory, at 150 meters, and the special observatory, at 250 meters, provide stunning views of the city, especially enchanting at night when Tokyo lights up like a vast, glittering sea. The tower's foot houses "FootTown," a multi-story complex with museums, restaurants, and shops, including One Piece Tower, an indoor theme park dedicated to the popular manga and anime series.

Choosing Your Experience: The choice between Skytree and Tokyo Tower often comes down to what you seek from your Tokyo visit. Skytree offers a glimpse into the future, a symbol of the city's high-tech aspirations and a gateway to cutting-edge entertainment. In contrast, Tokyo Tower offers a journey through time, a nostalgic trip to a Tokyo that has gracefully aged, yet stands firm as a beacon of hope and progress.

Beyond the Views: Both towers are more than just observation spots; they are cultural landmarks that offer a deeper understanding of Tokyo's heart and soul. Whether you're marveling at the technological marvel of the Skytree or soaking in the historical resonance of the Tokyo Tower, each visit leaves you with a sense of connection to the city's past, present, and future.

Skytree and Tokyo Tower reveals unique aspects that enhance your visit:

Seasonal Illuminations: Both landmarks feature seasonal lighting designs. Tokyo Tower's illumination often honors cultural events or causes, while Skytree's lighting can change color to mark special occasions or seasons, adding a festive touch to the skyline.

Cultural Events: Skytree hosts various events throughout the year, from art exhibitions to seasonal festivals, offering visitors a blend of modern culture with traditional Japanese celebrations.

Skytree's Tembo Deck and Galleria: Beyond the main observation areas, the Tembo Galleria offers a "walk in the sky" experience, allowing visitors to stroll at towering heights with the city sprawled below, offering a different perspective than the main decks.

Tokyo Tower's FootTown: The base of Tokyo Tower, FootTown, is not just about shopping and dining; it also hosts a Guinness World Records Museum and a Trick Art Gallery, providing a quirky and fun exploration space for families and groups.

Accessibility: Both landmarks are conveniently accessible via public transport, but their surrounding areas offer different vibes—Skytree is close to the historic Asakusa area, while Tokyo Tower is near the upscale Roppongi and Minato districts, influencing the choice depending on your itinerary.

Experiences of Skytree and Tokyo Tower without retracing steps, let's explore additional facets that distinguish each landmark:

Skytree's Sumida Aquarium: Located within the Tokyo Skytree Town complex, the Sumida Aquarium offers an immersive experience with its innovative tank designs and exhibitions, such as the tranquil jellyfish display and the indoor open pool that replicates the Tokyo Bay aquatic environment. It's a contrast to the technological marvel above, showcasing the natural beauty beneath the sea level.

Tokyo Tower's Shinto Shrine: At the base of Tokyo Tower lies a small Shinto shrine, adding a spiritual dimension to your visit. This juxtaposition of modern architecture with traditional spirituality is a unique aspect of Tokyo Tower, offering a moment of reflection amidst the urban exploration.

Skytree's Soramachi Shopping Complex: Beyond the typical mall, Soramachi includes a variety of traditional craft stores and artisanal shops, providing a platform for local craftspeople to showcase their work. It's an excellent place to find unique souvenirs that carry the essence of Japanese craftsmanship.

Tokyo Tower's Lookdown Window: For those seeking a thrill, Tokyo Tower's special observatory includes a lookdown window, a glass floor section that allows you to gaze directly down at the city from 250 meters up, offering a different kind of vertigo-inducing view compared to Skytree's enclosed observatories.

Dining Options with a View: Both landmarks boast restaurants that offer not just delicious meals but also panoramic views of Tokyo. Skytree's Sky Restaurant 634 (Musashi) provides French-Japanese fusion cuisine, while Tokyo Tower's Top Deck Restaurant offers a more intimate dining experience with the city lights sprawling beneath you.

Cultural Integration: Both Skytree and Tokyo Tower are not standalone attractions but are integrated into the fabric of their neighborhoods. Exploring around Skytree, you can visit the traditional crafts museum or the postal museum, while the area around Tokyo Tower is rich with embassies and cultural institutions, adding layers of cultural exploration to your visit.

THE EMPEROR'S HOME

Surrounded by moats and massive stone walls, lies the Imperial Palace, the primary residence of the Emperor of Japan. This majestic complex, with its lush gardens, historic buildings, and serene waterways, stands as a testament to Japan's enduring traditions and the imperial family's role in the heart of its capital.

Exploring the Grounds: The Imperial Palace is more than just a home; it's a sprawling estate that invites visitors to explore its outer gardens, which are open to the public throughout the year. The East Gardens, in particular, are a highlight, offering a tranquil escape with beautifully manicured lawns, traditional Japanese gardens, and the remnants of

Edo Castle's towers and moats, telling tales of a Tokyo before it became the metropolis it is today.

Seasonal Beauty: Each season adds a new dimension to the Imperial Palace's allure. The cherry blossoms of spring paint the gardens in soft pinks, drawing locals and visitors alike for hanami, the traditional cherry blossom viewing. Autumn brings a fiery palette of reds and oranges, offering a picturesque backdrop for leisurely walks through the palace's vast grounds.

Special Openings: While the inner grounds of the Imperial Palace are generally not open to the public, special openings on January 2nd (New Year's Greeting) and on the Emperor's birthday offer a rare opportunity to catch a glimpse of the imperial family and the inner palace courtyards, a moment where tradition and reverence fill the air.

Guided Tours: For those seeking deeper insights into the history and significance of the Imperial Palace, guided tours are available, providing access to parts of the inner palace grounds. These tours, often free of charge, offer a narrative to the complex's architectural marvels and historical importance, though they require advance booking.

Architectural Marvels: The Palace's architecture, a harmonious blend of traditional Japanese and modern styles, speaks volumes of the country's journey through the ages. The Nijubashi Bridge, with its iconic double arches, serves as the picturesque entrance to the inner palace, symbolizing the gateway between the modern city outside and the ancient world within.

The Imperial Palace's Significance: Visiting the Imperial Palace is not just about witnessing the beauty of its gardens or the grandeur of its architecture; it's about connecting with Japan's cultural heart. It's a place where history is preserved, traditions are revered, and the continuity of Japan's imperial lineage is celebrated amidst the ever-evolving landscape of Tokyo.

Photography Hotspots: While much of the palace is restricted, the outer gardens and the Nijubashi Bridge present iconic photography opportunities, capturing the essence of Japan's royal and cultural heritage against the Tokyo skyline.

Running Path: The area surrounding the Imperial Palace is a popular route for runners, offering a scenic loop of about 5 kilometers. It's a unique way to experience the palace's outer moats and walls while engaging in daily Tokyo life.

Kikyo-mon Gate: A lesser-known spot where visitors can see an outer gate up close, offering a sense of the palace's scale and the meticulous care taken in maintaining its traditional architecture.

Seasonal Flora: Beyond cherry blossoms, the Imperial Palace gardens are home to a variety of seasonal flowers and trees, including colorful azaleas in spring and ginkgo trees turning gold in autumn, each adding a different charm to the palace grounds throughout the year.

Kitanomaru Park: Adjacent to the East Gardens, this park is often quieter and houses the Budokan, a venue famous for martial arts, concerts, and events, adding a modern cultural dimension to the historical area.

THE FAMOUS SHIBUYA SCRAMBLE

The Shibuya Scramble, with its sprawling intersection and waves of humanity crisscrossing in every direction, captures the essence of the City. Here, amidst the neon glow and towering screens, lies not just a pedestrian crossing but a stage for the human drama of the city to unfold.

Experiencing the Scramble: Standing at the edge of the Shibuya Scramble, you're on the brink of participating in one of the most iconic urban experiences globally. As the traffic halts and the sea of humanity flows, there's a moment of sheer awe at the organized chaos. It's an orchestrated ballet of pedestrians, each step a testament to the city's living, breathing rhythm.

Best Views: To fully appreciate the Shibuya Scramble's grandeur, seek out the vantage points that offer an aerial view. The Shibuya Station's Hachiko Exit leads to a popular spot, while nearby cafes and buildings offer a perch to watch the flow of the crowd below. As night falls, these viewpoints become even more magical, with the intersection's lights reflecting the city's vibrant life.

Cultural Significance: Beyond its physical spectacle, the Shibuya Scramble is a cultural landmark. It's a place where trends are set, where youths gather to express themselves, and where moments of chance encounters can lead to lifelong stories. The surrounding Shibuya district, with its shops, entertainment venues, and eateries, pulsates with the energy of Japan's youth culture, making the Scramble the heart of Tokyo's contemporary narrative.

Photography and Filming: For enthusiasts and professionals alike, the Shibuya Scramble is a quintessential Tokyo shot. Capturing the intersection from above or within the crowd offers a glimpse into the city's soul. However, it's important to be mindful of the flow of people and respect privacy when aiming for the perfect shot.

Immersive Experience: To truly embrace the Shibuya Scramble, allow yourself to be swept along by the crowd, then pause at the center, if only for a second, to take in the enormity of the city and the moment. It's here, in the heart of the scramble, that Tokyo's energy is most palpable, a city always on the move, yet always connected.

Shibuya Scramble experience:

Interactive Art Installations: Occasionally, the area around Shibuya Scramble becomes a canvas for interactive art projects and digital displays that engage pedestrians, blending technology with public art.

Seasonal Decorations: During holidays and festivals, Shibuya Scramble and its surroundings are adorned with thematic decorations, adding an extra layer of excitement and visual appeal to the already vibrant atmosphere.

Social Media Spots: Certain corners and spots around the Scramble have gained fame on social media for their perfect framing of the crossing. Finding these can add a fun element to your visit, capturing iconic images of Tokyo life.

Nightlife and Entertainment: The area around Shibuya Scramble is a gateway to some of Tokyo's most lively bars, clubs, and live music venues, offering a glimpse into the city's nightlife once the sun sets.

Observation Decks: New buildings with public observation decks have opened in recent years, providing fresh perspectives on the scramble. These spots are perfect for those looking to capture the crossing without the crowds of the more well-known locations.

3.2 CULTURAL DEEP DIVE

ANCIENT SENSO-JI

Nestled in the historic Asakusa district, Senso-ji stands as Tokyo's oldest and most significant temple, a place where legends breathe, and the air is thick with the scent of incense and the resonance of centuries-old chants. Its towering red lantern and majestic gates have welcomed pilgrims and visitors alike since the 7th century, offering a passage back in time, to the very soul of ancient Tokyo.

The Legend: The story of Senso-ji begins with two fishermen who found a statue of Kannon, the goddess of mercy, in the nearby Sumida River. The temple was then constructed to honor her, becoming a site of pilgrimage and devotion, a narrative that continues to imbue the temple grounds with a sense of wonder and spirituality.

Exploring the Temple Grounds: Entering through the Kaminarimon (Thunder Gate), marked by its massive lantern, visitors are led down Nakamise Street, a lively shopping alley offering traditional snacks, crafts, and souvenirs. This path not only leads to the temple's inner sanctum but also serves as a journey through Japanese culture and craftsmanship.

The Main Hall and Pagoda: At the heart of Senso-ji, the Hozomon Gate opens up to the main hall (Hondo), a stunning example of Buddhist architecture, housing the revered Kannon statue, not visible to the public but represented by a golden image for worshippers to pray to. Adjacent stands a five-story pagoda, symbolizing the five elements of Buddhist cosmology, offering a picturesque backdrop that contrasts beautifully with the Tokyo Skytree in the distance.

Asakusa Shrine and Surroundings: Beside the main temple is the Asakusa Shrine, dedicated to the men who founded Senso-ji, celebrating the intertwining of divine intervention and human spirit. The surrounding gardens and smaller temples and shrines within the complex offer quiet corners for reflection, away from the bustling crowds.

Festivals and Events: Senso-ji is not just a monument to the past but a living, breathing cultural site. The annual Sanja Matsuri, one of Tokyo's largest and most vibrant festivals, transforms Asakusa into a spectacle of music, dance, and traditional costumes, celebrating the temple and its community.

A Moment of Reflection: Visiting Senso-ji offers more than just a cultural excursion; it invites a moment of personal reflection. Whether washing your hands and mouth at the chozuya, lighting an incense stick, or simply sitting and watching the devoted prayers, there's a palpable sense of connection to something greater, a thread linking the past to the present.

Essence of Senso-ji:

Omikuji Fortunes: At Senso-ji, visitors can experience drawing omikuji, traditional Japanese fortune-telling strips. Tied to trees or designated wires if they predict misfortune, it's a unique cultural experience that connects you with the hopes and rituals of both past and present visitors.

Nighttime Visit: Senso-ji presents a different atmosphere at night; the crowds dissipate, and the temple and pagoda are beautifully illuminated, offering a serene and almost mystical experience compared to the daytime bustle.

Asakusa Culture and Tourism Center: Just across from the Kaminarimon Gate, this center not only offers information and assistance to tourists but also features an observation deck with stunning views of the temple and the surrounding area, providing a modern architectural contrast to the ancient temple.

Nakamise Shopping Street: Beyond the typical souvenirs, Nakamise offers traditional snacks like ningyo-yaki (doll cakes) and senbei (rice crackers), giving visitors a taste of Edo-period street food.

Hidden Gems: Around the temple complex, smaller gardens and lesser-known halls, like the Zenizuka Jizo Hall, dedicated to the deity of good fortune and saving money, offer quiet spots for contemplation away from the main pathways.

These aspects of Senso-ji enhance the visit, offering a deeper dive into the temple's cultural significance and the surrounding area's offerings, making your travel more immersive experience.

PEACEFUL MEIJI SHRINE

Nestled within a sprawling forest that shields it from the city's hustle, Meiji Shrine is dedicated to the deified spirits of Emperor Meiji and his consort, Empress Shoken.

A Walk Through Nature: The approach to Meiji Shrine is unlike any other in Tokyo. A gravel path, shaded by towering trees over a century old, leads visitors into the heart of the shrine complex. The forest, composed of around 120,000 trees donated from regions across Japan, envelops you in an almost palpable serenity, making the walk itself a meditative experience.

Architectural Harmony: The shrine's architecture is a testament to understated elegance, embodying Shinto principles of simplicity and harmony with nature. Constructed using primarily cypress wood and copper, the buildings blend seamlessly into the surrounding forest, inviting a sense of calm and reverence.

Purification and Prayer: Upon reaching the shrine's entrance, visitors partake in a purification ritual at the temizuya, cleansing hands and mouth with water to prepare for a moment of prayer or reflection. The act is a symbolic gesture of leaving the mundane behind and entering a sacred space with a clear heart and mind.

Cultural Celebrations: Meiji Shrine is not just a place of quiet contemplation but also a vibrant center of cultural and spiritual life. Traditional Shinto weddings, often witnessed by visitors, are a beautiful spectacle of ritual and attire, offering a glimpse into the continuity of cultural practices. The shrine also hosts annual events, like the New Year's celebration and the spring and autumn festivals, connecting the community with its traditions.

Inner Garden and Treasures: Beyond the main shrine area, the Inner Garden is a place of particular beauty, especially during the irises' blooming season in June. Another hidden gem is the Treasure House, which displays personal belongings of Emperor Meiji and Empress Shoken, offering insights into their lives and the era they symbolize.

A Moment of Reflection: Visiting Meiji Shrine offers more than a break from the bustling city; it provides a moment of reflection on the values of peace, renewal, and the deep cultural roots that ground the fast-paced life of Tokyo. It's a reminder of the enduring spirit of Japan, a bridge between the past and the present, set within a sanctuary of nature.

Experience of Meiji Shrine, here are some unique insights:

Nature's Symphony: Early morning visits to Meiji Shrine offer a unique opportunity to hear a captivating "symphony" created by the diverse bird species residing in the surrounding forest. This natural melody, combined with the serene atmosphere, provides a profoundly peaceful start to the day.

Kiyomasa's Well: Hidden within the shrine's grounds is Kiyomasa's Well, named after a famous samurai and known for its clear, purifying waters. This spot is considered to have strong spiritual energy and is a favorite among those seeking contemplation and renewal.

Sake Barrels: Near the shrine's entrance, visitors are greeted by rows of colorful sake barrels, donated by breweries from across Japan as offerings to the deified spirits of Emperor Meiji and his consort. These barrels, or "kazaridaru," symbolize prosperity and peace, and their vibrant designs add a unique cultural and visual element to the shrine's entrance.

Poetry and Nature: Emperor Meiji was known for his love of poetry, particularly waka poems. The shrine occasionally displays some of his poems, offering insights into his thoughts and philosophies, many of which reflect a deep appreciation for nature and harmony.

Seasonal Beauty: The shrine's landscape is meticulously designed to showcase the beauty of each season. Apart from the irises in June, the autumn months bring a stunning display of fall foliage, transforming the shrine's surroundings into a tapestry of warm colors, further enhancing the spiritual and aesthetic experience for visitors.

3.3 ONLY IN TOKYO

CATCH A SUMO MATCH

Sumo, Japan's national sport, is an experience that embodies the essence of Japanese culture, strength, and honor.

The Heart of Sumo: The Ryogoku Kokugikan in Tokyo is the heart of the sumo world. This arena hosts three of the six annual Grand Sumo Tournaments, making it the best place to catch a match and feel the earth-shaking intensity of the bouts. Each tournament spans 15 days, offering ample opportunity to witness the power and ceremony of sumo.

Understanding Sumo: Sumo is more than a test of strength; it's a ritualistic performance that includes elements of Shinto tradition. Matches are preceded by elaborate rituals - from the salt-throwing to purify the ring, to the ceremonial leg stomping to drive away evil spirits. Understanding these rituals adds depth to the spectacle, revealing the sport's rich cultural significance.

Attending a Tournament: Securing tickets to a sumo tournament requires planning, especially for seats close to the action. Tickets can be purchased online or at the venue, but for popular matches, it's wise to book in advance. Once inside, you're not just a spectator; you're part of an age-old tradition, enveloped in the crowd's gasps and cheers as these titanic athletes clash.

The Sumo Experience: Beyond the matches, visiting Ryogoku Kokugikan offers a chance to explore sumo's history at the Sumo Museum located within the complex. Exhibitions display sumo artifacts, costumes, and portraits of legendary wrestlers, providing a deeper understanding of the sport's evolution and its heroes.

Sumo Stables: For those seeking an even closer look at sumo, visits to sumo stables, where wrestlers live and train, can be arranged. Observing a morning practice session is a rare privilege, offering insights into the wrestlers' rigorous training regimes and the discipline that shapes their lives.

Culinary Side of Sumo: Completing the sumo experience, indulge in chanko-nabe, the hearty stew that sumo wrestlers eat to build mass and strength. Many restaurants around Ryogoku serve this protein-rich dish, allowing you to taste a piece of sumo culture.

Catching a sumo match in Tokyo is an unforgettable experience that connects you directly to the heart of Japanese culture. It's a spectacle of strength, tradition, and ceremony that stays with you long after the final bout is won.

Sumo in Tokyo further reveals unique aspects for an enriching experience:

Sumo Morning Practice: Some sumo stables allow visitors to watch morning practice sessions, known as "asageiko." It's a rare opportunity to see the wrestlers' training up close, showcasing their dedication and discipline. Remember, strict etiquette is observed, and prior arrangements are often required.

Sumo Museum: Located within the Ryogoku Kokugikan Sumo Arena, the Sumo Museum collects and displays a wide range of sumo-related artifacts. The exhibits, which rotate several times a year, provide insights into the history and cultural significance of sumo through ancient scrolls, elaborate costumes, and portraits of famous sumo wrestlers.

Seasonal Availability: The Grand Sumo Tournaments in Tokyo are held in January, May, and September. Planning your visit around these times not only guarantees the sumo experience but also allows you to enjoy Tokyo's seasonal attractions.

Sumo Wrestler Sightings: For those visiting the Ryogoku area, even outside tournament times, it's not uncommon to encounter sumo wrestlers going about their daily lives. The local neighborhood is deeply connected to the sumo culture, offering a more personal glimpse into the world of sumo.

Regional Tournaments and Exhibitions: Beyond the major tournaments, sumo exhibitions and regional tours occur throughout the year, offering additional opportunities to witness sumo matches. These events, though smaller, provide a closer look at the sport in a more intimate setting.

SING YOUR HEART OUT: KARAOKE

It's an immersive experience that epitomizes the joy of sharing moments with friends, family, or even strangers who become friends by the song's end.

The Karaoke Box Phenomenon: Unlike the open-mic setup familiar in many countries, Tokyo specializes in karaoke boxes – private rooms that you rent by the hour, offering a personal and intimate setting where groups can let loose away from the public eye. These venues range from the luxuriously themed to the cozily simple, catering to all preferences and occasions.

Choosing Your Venue: Tokyo's districts each offer a unique karaoke experience. Shibuya and Shinjuku are pulsating with neon-lit karaoke buildings where the latest hits and classic tracks echo into the night. In contrast, quieter neighborhoods offer more laid-back venues, perfect for those looking to sing in a more relaxed atmosphere.

Technological Marvels: The karaoke experience in Tokyo is enhanced by state-of-the-art technology. Touchscreen interfaces allow you to search for songs by title, artist, or even by typing in lyrics. Many venues offer multilingual systems, ensuring non-Japanese speakers can easily navigate through thousands of songs in various languages.

Beyond Singing: Modern karaoke establishments in Tokyo offer a plethora of additional services – from costume rentals that let you transform into your favorite pop stars to extensive food and drink menus that ensure your group stays energized for hours of singing. Some even offer recording services, so you can take home a souvenir of your musical escapades.

Cultural Integration: Engaging in karaoke in Tokyo is more than just entertainment; it's a window into the Japanese way of bonding and communal enjoyment. It's common for business colleagues, friends, and families to gather in karaoke boxes as a way to celebrate, unwind, and strengthen relationships.

Making the Most of Your Karaoke Night: To truly embrace the karaoke culture in Tokyo, let go of inhibitions and dive into the experience. Whether belting out ballads, pop hits, or duets, karaoke is about joy, laughter, and the occasional off-key note. It's about creating a soundtrack to your Tokyo adventure, one song at a time.

Here are some unique insights to enhance your experience:

Late-Night Options: Many karaoke venues in Tokyo operate 24/7, making it a popular after-hours activity. Some spots offer "all-night" packages, perfect for those who want to sing until the sun comes up.

Drink and Snack Packages: To complement your singing session, karaoke boxes often provide food and drink packages. From soft drinks and snacks to full-course meals and unlimited drinks, these packages cater to all tastes and help keep the party going.

Theme Rooms: For a unique karaoke experience, look for venues offering themed rooms.

From pop idol stages to tropical beaches and even horror-themed rooms, these special settings add an extra layer of fun to your karaoke night.

Solo Karaoke: For solo travelers or those looking to practice their singing in private, "hitokara" (solo karaoke) booths are available in some venues. These smaller rooms offer a comfortable space to enjoy karaoke alone.

Karaoke Competitions: Some karaoke venues host competitions or "karaoke battles," where singers can showcase their talents and compete with others. Participating in or watching one of these contests can be an exciting way to experience the competitive side of karaoke culture.

RELAX IN A JAPANESE HOT SPRING

While a modern metropolis, it is blessed with natural hot springs, allowing residents and visitors alike to dip into the ancient wellness practices of Japan. These onsens are not just about bathing; they are cultural institutions, offering a glimpse into a lifestyle that cherishes balance, wellness, and harmony with nature.

Urban Onsens: Nestled within the city's heart are several urban onsens that capture the essence of this tradition. These facilities blend the natural hot spring experience with the convenience of city life, offering outdoor and indoor baths, sauna rooms, and sometimes even spa treatments. From the historic to the contemporary, each onsen has its unique charm, providing a peaceful retreat amid the urban hustle.

Experiencing a Traditional Onsen: The onsen ritual is as much about the mind as it is about the body. Before entering the bath, you're expected to wash thoroughly at the provided shower stations, embracing cleanliness and respect for others. Once prepared, you step into the soothing waters, where the heat envelops you, melting away the stresses of the day. It's a moment of quiet reflection, a pause that reconnects you with the present.

Public Baths and Private Experiences: For those seeking solitude or perhaps a romantic getaway, many onsens offer private baths. These can be reserved for individual or small group use, providing a personal space to enjoy the hot spring waters in complete privacy.

Therapeutic Waters: The waters of Tokyo's onsens are rich in minerals, each with different health benefits, from improving skin conditions to relieving muscle pain. The experience is not just a bath but a healing ritual that nurtures both body and spirit.

Onsen Etiquette: Understanding onsen etiquette enhances the experience. Tattoos, for example, are traditionally frowned upon in many onsens due to associations with yakuza (organized crime). However, some places are more lenient or offer cover-up stickers. Silence or whispers are appreciated, maintaining the tranquil atmosphere.

Seasonal Enjoyment: While onsens can be enjoyed year-round, each season offers a distinct experience. Winter, with its crisp air, makes the steaming baths even more magical, while spring and autumn baths are accompanied by the beauty of cherry blossoms and fall foliage, respectively.

Relaxing in a Japanese hot spring in Tokyo offers an oasis of calm, a tradition that flows deep through Japan's cultural landscape.

Night Bathing: Some hot springs in Tokyo offer night bathing experiences, allowing visitors to soak under the stars, adding a serene and almost mystical quality to the onsen experience.

Foot Baths: For those short on time or not ready for a full onsen experience, foot baths (ashiyu) offer a quick and relaxing way to enjoy hot spring benefits. They're common in neighborhoods with natural hot springs and some urban onsen complexes.

Salt Saunas: A unique feature of some Tokyo onsens is the salt sauna, where visitors can rub mineral-rich salt on their skin before entering the sauna, enhancing the detoxifying and skin-improving effects of the heat.

Seasonal Specials: Many onsens in Tokyo incorporate seasonal elements into their baths, such as yuzu (Japanese citrus) baths in winter, which are believed to warm the body and protect the skin.

Cultural Workshops: Beyond the bath, some onsen facilities host cultural workshops or offer traditional dining experiences, providing a more holistic introduction to Japanese traditions alongside the hot spring visit.

3.4 FOOD LOVER'S TOKYO

SUSHI AND RAMEN SECRETS

Sushi - The Art of Simplicity: In Tokyo, sushi transforms from a mere dish to an art form. The city's sushi ranges from conveyor belt kaiten-zushi to exclusive, Michelin-starred establishments. The secret lies in the rice, seasoned with a balance of vinegar, sugar, and salt, coupled with the freshest fish, often sourced from the legendary Tsukiji Outer Market. Master sushi chefs spend years, sometimes decades, perfecting their craft, focusing on the temperature, texture, and balance of flavors. For an immersive experience, visit a sushi bar where you can watch the chef at work, each slice and roll a testament to years of dedication.

Ramen - A Bowl Full of Soul: Ramen in Tokyo is as diverse as the city itself, with each region represented through its unique broth and noodle combination. From the rich, creamy tonkotsu broth of Kyushu to the soy-based shoyu ramen of Tokyo, each bowl tells a story. Secret tip: look out for the small, often inconspicuous shops, where long queues signal a culinary treasure waiting to be discovered. These places often specialize in a single type of ramen, perfected over time. Don't miss experimenting with different toppings, such as ajitama (soft-boiled seasoned egg), nori, and chashu (braised pork belly), to customize your bowl.

Seasonal and Regional Varieties: Both sushi and ramen offer seasonal specialties that reflect the diversity of Japan's climates and waters. For sushi, spring brings sakura-ebi (cherry blossom shrimp), while autumn introduces rich, fatty tuna. Ramen, on the other hand, adapts its broths and ingredients to the season, offering lighter options in summer and heartier, warming bowls in winter.

Learning from the Masters: For those seeking a deeper understanding, Tokyo offers sushi and ramen making classes taught by seasoned chefs. These classes provide insight into the techniques and traditions behind these dishes, from cooking the perfect sushi rice to preparing your own ramen broth from scratch.

Tasting Tours: Embark on a guided food tour to explore the hidden gems of Tokyo's sushi and ramen scene. These tours often include visits to several eateries, each highlighting a different aspect of the dishes' culinary diversity, along with insights into the history and culture of Japanese cuisine.

Sushi and ramen are more than just food; they are cultural experiences that encapsulate the essence of Japan's culinary philosophy.

Early Morning Sushi: For the freshest experience, consider visiting a sushi restaurant early in the morning, especially those near fish markets. It's a tradition for many locals and chefs to enjoy sushi for breakfast, capturing the peak freshness of seafood.

Regional Ramen Variants Within Tokyo: Tokyo is a melting pot of regional ramen variants from across Japan. Look out for specialty shops that focus on specific styles, such as Hokkaido's miso ramen or Hakata's tonkotsu, offering a taste tour of Japan's diverse ramen culture without leaving the city.

Sushi Etiquette: When eating sushi, it's customary to use your hands for nigiri (sliced fish over rice) and to dip the fish side into the soy sauce, not the rice, to avoid breaking apart the delicate piece or soaking the rice too much.

Customizing Ramen: Many ramen shops in Tokyo allow you to customize your order to your preference, including the level of broth richness, noodle firmness, and the amount of garlic or spice. This customization is part of the ramen experience, catering to individual tastes.

Standing Sushi Bars: For a quick and authentic sushi experience, visit one of Tokyo's standing sushi bars. These establishments offer high-quality sushi at a fraction of the price of sit-down restaurants, perfect for diners on the go.

Here are more tips to enhance your sushi and ramen adventure:

Late-Night Ramen: Tokyo's nightlife isn't complete without a visit to a ramen shop post-midnight. These late-night bowls serve not just as comfort food but also as a window into the city's round-the-clock lifestyle. Some of the best ramen experiences can be found in the wee hours, offering a savory end to a night out.

Sushi at Local Markets: Aside from the well-known fish markets, local neighborhood markets sometimes host hidden sushi gems. These stalls often have their own loyal following and offer an intimate sushi dining experience, where the chef prepares each piece directly in front of you, often engaging in friendly conversation.

Ramen Toppings on the Side: When exploring Tokyo's ramen scene, don't hesitate to order extra toppings on the side. This allows you to customize your bowl as you eat, adding ingredients like bamboo shoots, green onions, or extra slices of pork to suit your taste and texture preferences.

Soy Sauce Wisdom: With sushi, the use of soy sauce can be a delicate matter. In high-end sushi restaurants, the chef might season each piece perfectly, negating the need for extra soy sauce. Observing others or politely asking the chef for guidance can enhance your sushi etiquette and overall experience.

Discovering Soba and Udon: While diving into sushi and ramen, don't overlook Tokyo's soba (buckwheat noodles) and udon (thick wheat noodles) scenes. These noodles offer different textures and flavors, often served in a variety of hot and cold dishes, providing a broader taste of traditional Japanese cuisine.

Sustainable Seafood: As global awareness of ocean conservation grows, some sushi restaurants in Tokyo emphasize sustainable seafood practices. These establishments can offer a unique perspective on the future of sushi, combining traditional techniques with modern environmental consciousness.

Secret Menus and Seasonal Specials: In both sushi and ramen shops, asking about secret menus or seasonal specials can unveil unique dishes not listed on the regular menu, offering a taste of the chef's creativity and seasonal ingredients at their peak.

STREET SNACKS AND PUB GRUBS

The Allure of Street Snacks: Tokyo's streets are a canvas of culinary delights, offering an array of snacks that tantalize the taste buds and ignite the senses. From the sweet, fluffy texture of taiyaki, a fish-shaped cake filled with red bean paste, to the savory crunch of takoyaki, octopus-filled dough balls topped with tangy sauce and bonito flakes, each snack is a bite-sized journey through Tokyo's diverse flavors. The exploration continues with yakitori (grilled chicken skewers) sizzling at street stalls, each piece carefully turned until perfectly charred, embodying the simple yet profound pleasure of street dining.

Izakaya - Japan's Pub Culture: The izakaya experience is Tokyo's answer to the pub, offering a casual setting where food and drink share the spotlight. These establishments, ranging from tiny, intimate spaces to larger, lively venues, serve an eclectic mix of dishes designed to complement the drinking experience. Here, the ritual of sharing small plates, from sizzling karaage (fried chicken) to refreshing cucumber with miso, fosters a sense of community and conviviality. It's in these moments, amid the clinking of glasses and the chorus of "kanpai" (cheers), that the essence of Tokyo's social dining culture comes alive.

Exploring Yokocho Alleys: Tucked away in Tokyo's bustling neighborhoods are yokocho alleys, narrow lanes lined with small eateries and bars, each with its own character. These alleys offer an immersive experience into Tokyo's nightlife, where the glow of paper lanterns and the aroma of grilled meats fill the air. Venturing into a yokocho, like the famous Omoide Yokocho in Shinjuku or Ebisu Yokocho, is a step into the heart of Tokyo's dining culture, where every stall has a story, and every dish reflects a piece of the city's culinary soul.

The Craft of Beverages: Complementing Tokyo's street snacks and pub grubs is the art of Japanese beverages. From the smooth, umami-rich sake served in izakayas to the craft beers that have taken the city by storm, Tokyo offers a drink for every palate. Exploring local breweries or sake bars allows one to delve deeper into the craft behind these beverages, each sip a testament to Tokyo's dedication to quality and tradition.

Late-Night Eats: Tokyo's culinary scene thrives at night, when the city's chefs and food vendors cater to night owls and revelers seeking sustenance. This is the time to discover ramen joints that stay open until the early hours, serving steaming bowls of broth and noodles, or to find a 24-hour gyudon (beef bowl) restaurant, offering comfort food at any hour.

STREET SNACKS

Menchi Katsu: A beloved street snack, menchi katsu is a breaded and deep-fried patty made from ground meat and onions. Juicy on the inside and crispy on the outside, it's often served with a tangy tonkatsu sauce, making it a satisfying comfort food that perfectly encapsulates the fusion of Western and Japanese culinary traditions.

Yakisoba: Often found sizzling on large griddles at street festivals, yakisoba is a stir-fried noodle dish mixed with bite-sized pork, vegetables, and a sweet and savory sauce. Served piping hot, often in a paper plate with pickled ginger and aonori (green seaweed powder) on top, it's a quintessential taste of Tokyo's outdoor culinary scene.

Dango: For those with a sweet tooth, dango, skewered rice dumplings, are a must-try. These chewy treats are typically glazed with a sweet soy sauce or covered in a sweet and savory kinako (roasted soybean flour), offering a simple yet profound flavor that reflects the minimalist beauty of Japanese sweets.

Imagawayaki: Another sweet snack, imagawayaki is a round, filled cake that resembles taiyaki but with a thicker batter. Common fillings include red bean paste, custard, or sweet potato, making it a popular choice during festivals or as a comforting street-side treat.

Street Crepes: A twist on a French classic, Tokyo's street crepes are rolled into a cone and filled with a variety of sweet options, from fresh fruit and whipped cream to chocolate and ice cream. Found in trendy neighborhoods like Harajuku, these crepes have become a symbol of Tokyo's youthful energy and its embrace of global culinary influences.

Tokyo's Izakaya: A Culinary Adventure

Understanding Izakaya Culture: The izakaya experience is quintessentially Japanese, focusing on the joy of sharing. Dishes are typically served in small portions, designed to be enjoyed communally, fostering a sense of togetherness. From the moment you slide open the door and are greeted with a chorus of "Irasshaimase!" (Welcome!), you're invited into a world where food and drink harmonize to create unforgettable memories.

Signature Dishes to Explore: The magic of izakaya lies in its diverse menu, offering everything from simple edamame (boiled soybeans) sprinkled with salt to complex dishes like yakitori (grilled chicken skewers), perfectly charred and seasoned. Here are some must-try dishes:

Sashimi: Fresh slices of raw fish, a testament to the Japanese pursuit of simplicity and perfection.

Takoyaki: Ball-shaped snacks filled with minced octopus, a popular choice for something warm and comforting.

Karaage: Japanese-style fried chicken, marinated and coated in a light batter, offering a crispy exterior and juicy interior.

Grilled Fish: Seasonal fish grilled to perfection, highlighting the natural flavors of the sea.

Tofu Dishes: Soft, silken tofu topped with bonito flakes and soy sauce, a dish that celebrates the delicate flavors of its ingredients.

Pairing with Drinks: No izakaya experience is complete without the careful selection of beverages. Sake, with its nuanced flavors, is a classic choice, offering a smooth complement to both the light and rich dishes. Beer, crisp and refreshing, is another staple, perfect for toasting to good health and good company. For those looking for something different, shochu, a distilled spirit, and umeshu, a sweet plum wine, provide a deeper dive into Japan's alcoholic beverages.

Navigating Tokyo's Izakaya Scene: Tips for the Uninitiated

Reservations and Etiquette: While many izakayas welcome walk-ins, making a reservation can ensure your spot, especially in popular establishments. Upon entering, it's customary to remove your shoes if tatami seating is offered, embracing the traditional aspect of izakaya dining.

Navigating the Menu: Menus can be extensive and sometimes only in Japanese. Don't hesitate to ask the staff for recommendations; many izakayas are known for their specialty dishes or seasonal offerings. Picture menus and English translations are becoming more common, aiding in the selection process.

All-You-Can-Eat and Drink Options: Some izakayas offer "nomihoudai" (all-you-can-drink) and "tabehoudai" (all-you-can-eat) options, providing a fixed price for a set time limit. This can be a great way to sample a variety of dishes and drinks, but be mindful of the time restrictions and the etiquette of not wasting food.

The Art of Ordering: Start with a few dishes and order progressively, mirroring the izakaya's pacing and giving you the chance to explore a broader range of the menu. It's also a way to gauge portion sizes, which can vary from one izakaya to another.

Ending Your Meal: Concluding your izakaya experience with a rice or noodle dish is traditional, signifying the end of the meal. Whether it's a comforting bowl of miso soup with clams or a hearty serving of oyakodon (chicken and egg rice bowl), this final dish helps to round out the evening.

Payment: Check if the izakaya has a table charge, known as "otoshi" or "tsukidashi," which is a small cover charge that sometimes includes a small appetizer. Payment is typically made at the counter when leaving, and splitting the bill is common practice among friends.

Modern Izakayas and Fusion Dishes: In recent years, Tokyo has seen the rise of modern izakayas that blend traditional Japanese pub grub with global culinary trends, creating innovative dishes that challenge and delight the palate. From tapas-style small plates featuring international flavors to creative vegan adaptations of classic izakaya dishes, these establishments cater to a diverse and adventurous clientele.

Specialty Izakayas: Beyond the generalist izakaya, Tokyo boasts specialty izakayas focused on particular ingredients or cooking styles. Seafood izakayas, for example, offer a dazzling array of fish and shellfish, often sourced directly from local markets, prepared in myriad ways. Similarly, yakitori izakayas dedicate their menus to the art of grilled chicken, exploring every conceivable cut and marination.

Seasonal and Local Ingredients: Emphasizing the Japanese principle of "shun," which celebrates seasonal produce, many izakayas adjust their menus to feature the freshest ingredients available throughout the year. This commitment to seasonality not only supports local farmers and fisheries but also ensures a dining experience that is both varied and reflective of Japan's rich culinary heritage.

Craft Beers and Sake Pairings: As the craft beer movement has taken root in Tokyo, many izakayas have begun to offer an impressive selection of local and international craft beers, providing a perfect complement to the savory flavors of pub grub. Likewise, the art of sake pairing, selecting the right type of sake to enhance the flavors of the food, has become a refined practice in many establishments, elevating the dining experience.

Interactive Dining Experiences: Some izakayas enhance the communal dining experience by incorporating interactive elements, such as DIY grilling at your table or self-service beer taps. These interactive experiences add a fun and engaging dimension to the meal, encouraging diners to participate actively in the preparation of their food.

Local Hangouts and Hidden Gems: Beyond the well-trodden tourist paths, Tokyo's neighborhoods are dotted with small, local izakayas that serve as community hangouts. These hidden gems, often passed down through generations, offer an authentic glimpse into the everyday dining culture of Tokyo's residents, serving classic dishes in a warm and welcoming atmosphere.

NAVIGATING TOKYO'S CULINARY SCENE WITH DIETARY NEEDS

Vegetarian and Vegan Options: Vegetarian and vegan dining has blossomed in recent years, with a growing number of eateries dedicated to plant-based cuisine. From traditional Japanese dishes reimagined without animal products to modern cafes serving up global vegetarian and vegan fare, Tokyo is proving that its culinary innovation knows no bounds. Key neighborhoods like Shibuya and Shinjuku have become hotspots for vegetarian and vegan restaurants, offering everything from veggie ramen and sushi to plant-based burgers.

Gluten-Free Guidance: For those navigating gluten sensitivities or celiac disease, Tokyo's food scene can be challenging, given the prevalence of soy sauce and other wheat-based ingredients in Japanese cooking. However, the city is becoming more aware of gluten-free diets, with some restaurants now offering gluten-free dishes or even entire menus. Specialty shops and health food stores also stock gluten-free soy sauce and other essentials, making it easier for gluten-free travelers to explore Tokyo's culinary delights without worry.

Halal and Kosher Options: As Tokyo has grown more cosmopolitan, so too has its accommodation of diverse dietary laws. Halal and kosher food options are increasingly available, particularly in areas with international communities. Halal-certified restaurants and even some halal-friendly street food stalls cater to Muslim travelers, while a handful of establishments offer kosher meals, ensuring that dietary observances are respected.

Allergen Awareness: Japan's meticulous approach to food extends to allergen labeling, with packaged foods often clearly marked for common allergens. In restaurants, don't hesitate to ask about ingredients, as many chefs are accommodating once they understand your needs. Carrying an allergy card in Japanese, detailing your specific allergies, can be a helpful tool in ensuring your dietary needs are clearly communicated.

Navigating Traditional Cuisine: Traditional Japanese cuisine, with its emphasis on seasonal ingredients and natural flavors, offers many dishes that can be enjoyed by those with dietary restrictions. Soba (buckwheat noodles), for instance, is a delightful option for those avoiding gluten (just be sure to confirm that the soba is 100% buckwheat and ask for gluten-free soy sauce). Similarly, tofu and other soy products provide a protein-rich choice for vegetarians and vegans.

Specialty Stores and Supermarkets: Supermarkets and health food stores are treasure troves for those with dietary needs. Organic and natural food stores, increasingly common in the city, offer a range of products catering to various dietary requirements. International supermarkets also stock a variety of imported goods, providing familiar options for travelers.

Dining Etiquette and Communication: When dining out, clear communication is key. While English is not universally spoken, many restaurants in Tokyo have English menus or picture menus that can aid in your selection. Expressing your dietary needs politely and showing appreciation for any accommodations made can go a long way in ensuring a pleasant dining experience for both you and the establishment.

Experience and Exploration: Food scene with dietary needs is not just about finding places that can cater to you but also about exploring and experiencing the city's culinary diversity within your dietary boundaries. Engaging with Tokyo's food culture—be it through a cooking class, a food tour with a focus on dietary-aware offerings, or simply by trying new dishes within your dietary framework—is a journey that promises both challenge and reward.

Here's the lowdown on some rad tips and spots that might not be on everyone's radar yet:

Pop-up Vegan Spots: Tokyo's got this growing trend of pop-up vegan spots that show up in the most unexpected places, like art galleries or clothing stores. Keep an eye on social media to catch these fleeting, super Instagrammable foodie experiences.

App Assistance: There are some awesome apps out there designed to help you navigate dietary restrictions in Japan. Apps like "HappyCow" can be a lifesaver in Tokyo, pointing you to the nearest vegan or vegetarian restaurants.

Local Vegan Festivals: Tokyo hosts some cool vegan festivals and markets from time to time, where you can try a bunch of different foods, all animal-free. It's not just about the food; it's a whole vibe, with music, workshops, and talks.

Ramen Hacks: For the gluten-free crew, ramen can be tricky, but some spots offer rice noodles as an alternative. And if you're vegan or vegetarian, look out for miso or vegetable-based broth options. Don't be shy to ask!

Conveyor Belt Sushi for Everyone: Yes, even sushi spots are getting with the times. Some conveyor belt sushi restaurants now offer clearly labeled vegetarian and vegan options, so you can grab plates without having to guess what's in each dish.

Drink Up: When it comes to drinks, Tokyo's scene is also getting more inclusive. You can find places serving non-alcoholic versions of classic Japanese drinks, so everyone can enjoy a night out without missing out on the fun.

Sweet Treats: Tokyo's dessert game is strong, and now there are more dairy-free and gluten-free options than ever. From traditional Japanese sweets to trendy dessert cafes, there's something for every sweet tooth.

3.5 SHOPPING SPREE

TECH AND ANIME LOOT

Akihabara: The Electric Town: Akihabara, affectionately known as Akiba, is the undisputed king of tech shopping in Tokyo. Its streets are lined with stores ranging from towering electronics retailers to specialized boutiques, offering everything from the latest in high-tech gadgets to rare, vintage finds. Here, you can get hands-on with the newest game consoles, cutting-edge robotics, and audiophile-grade sound systems. The district is also a hotspot for "otaku" culture, making it the perfect place to hunt for anime, manga, and video game loot alongside your tech haul.

Nakano Broadway: A lesser-known gem compared to Akihabara but no less fascinating, Nakano Broadway is a haven for collectors. This shopping complex is crammed with shops selling manga, anime figures, and vintage toys. It's also known for its selection of niche electronics and DIY tech kits, appealing to both hobbyists and those looking for unique tech-related souvenirs.

Shinjuku's Tech Giants: Shinjuku, with its futuristic skyline, is home to flagship stores of Japan's leading electronics brands. These multi-story tech palaces are where you can explore the latest innovations from Japan's tech industry, from ultra-thin OLED TVs to smart appliances that seem straight out of a sci-fi movie. Shinjuku's blend of tech and style makes it a must-visit for those wanting to experience the sleek side of Tokyo's electronics scene.

Anime Dreams Come to Life

Anime Centers and Cafes: Tokyo is filled with specialty stores and themed cafes dedicated to popular anime and manga series. From the Gundam Cafe to the Pokémon Center, these spots offer exclusive merchandise and a themed dining experience that immerses you in the worlds of your favorite characters. It's not just shopping; it's stepping into a scene from your beloved series.

Mandarake: For the ultimate anime and manga treasure hunt, Mandarake is the place to be. With several locations across Tokyo, the largest being in Akihabara, Mandarake specializes in pre-owned manga, anime DVDs, and collectibles. It's a labyrinth of nostalgia and rare finds, where each shelf is packed with stories waiting to be discovered.

Anime Street Art and Murals: Exploring Tokyo's tech and anime districts offers more than just shopping opportunities; it's a visual journey. Areas like Akihabara are adorned with colorful street art and murals depicting iconic anime scenes and characters, providing a vibrant backdrop to your shopping adventure.

Tips for the Ultimate Tech and Anime Shopping Experience

Bargain Hunting: While Tokyo's tech shops and anime stores are known for their vast selections, savvy shoppers know to look out for deals. Many stores offer tax-free shopping for tourists, and exploring the back streets of Akihabara can lead to second-hand shops with significant discounts on electronics and collectibles.

Language Barrier: Not all shops in Tokyo's tech and anime districts have English-speaking staff, but don't let that deter you. Many have signs and product descriptions in English, and smartphone translation apps can be invaluable tools for communication.

Cultural Etiquette: When shopping in Tokyo, especially for rare or collectible items, be mindful of the local shopping etiquette. Asking politely before taking photos in stores and handling merchandise with care are signs of respect that are appreciated by shop owners and staff.

Join a Guided Tour: For those who want to dive deep into Tokyo's tech and anime culture but don't know where to start, joining a guided tour can be a great option. These tours often provide insider knowledge, from the history of Akihabara's rise as an electronics hub to hidden spots where you can find the best anime merchandise.

Exploring Beyond the Mainstream: Beyond the well-trodden paths of Akihabara and Shinjuku, Tokyo is dotted with smaller neighborhoods and shops that cater to specific niches within the tech and anime worlds. From retro gaming bars to indie manga shops, there's a whole other layer of Tokyo to explore for those willing to venture off the beaten path.

Here's the lowdown on some cool spots and tips that might not be on every traveler's radar:

Virtual Reality (VR) Zones: Tokyo is on another level when it comes to VR experiences. Places like VR Zone Shinjuku offer mind-blowing games and experiences that aren't just about gaming; they're immersive adventures. It's like stepping into your favorite game or anime world for real.

Subculture Fashion Streets: For anime fans who also dig the fashion inspired by their favorite series, areas like Harajuku and Shibuya are goldmines. You'll find everything from cosplay outfits to streetwear inspired by anime characters. It's a cool way to see how Tokyo's youth culture blends fashion with fandom.

Anime Music Stores: If you're into anime, you know the music is a big deal. Tokyo has stores dedicated entirely to anime soundtracks and pop culture music. These spots often have listening stations, so you can jam out before deciding what to take home.

Figure Customization Shops: Beyond buying figures, Tokyo has places where you can customize your own or even take part in workshops to create or paint figures. It's a hands-on way to get even more into the anime world.

Otaku Bars and Cafes: While themed cafes are well-known, Tokyo also has its fair share of otaku bars – small, intimate places where fans gather to geek out over anime, manga, and games over drinks. It's a cool way to meet locals who share your interests.

Anime Pilgrimages: For the hardcore fans, Tokyo and its surroundings are full of real-life locations featured in popular anime. Doing an "anime pilgrimage" to visit these spots can be a fun and unique way to explore the city and see it through a different lens.

Tokyo's tech and anime culture is always evolving, with new spots popping up and hidden gems waiting to be discovered.

TRENDSETTING FASHION FINDS

Harajuku: The Birthplace of Kawaii: Harajuku isn't just a place; it's a phenomenon. As the birthplace of the kawaii (cute) culture, it embodies the spirit of youthful rebellion against traditional fashion norms. Takeshita Street, a narrow alleyway crammed with boutiques, vintage stores, and crepe stands, is where you'll find everything from gothic lolita dresses to the latest streetwear. It's a place where you're encouraged to express yourself, to mix and match, and to embrace the unconventional.

Shibuya: The Pulse of Youth Culture: Shibuya, with its iconic Scramble Crossing, is the heartbeat of Tokyo's youth culture. The area around Shibuya 109, a towering shopping mall dedicated to women's fashion, is a testament to the ever-evolving trends of the city's young population. Here, fashion is fast, bold, and unabashedly forward-thinking, offering a glimpse into the future of global trends.

Omotesando and Aoyama: High-End Haunts: For a more refined shopping experience, the tree-lined avenues of Omotesando and Aoyama are home to flagship stores of both international designers and renowned Japanese brands. This is where architecture meets fashion, with beautifully designed spaces showcasing minimalist Japanese aesthetics and cutting-edge fashion. It's a place to witness how Tokyo elegantly bridges the gap between its rich cultural heritage and its passion for modernity.

Daikanyama and Nakameguro: The Chic Side Streets: Away from the bustle of Tokyo's more famous shopping districts, Daikanyama and Nakameguro offer a laid-back vibe with a sophisticated edge. These neighborhoods are filled with boutique shops, second-hand stores, and designer outlets that cater to a discerning clientele looking for unique pieces that speak of individuality and elegance.

Navigating Tokyo's Fashion Wonderland

Street Style Inspirations: One of Tokyo's greatest fashion shows happens on the streets. Each district has its own vibe, from the eclectic and colorful ensembles of Harajuku to the sleek, monochromatic looks of Ginza. Take time to observe and draw inspiration from the people you see; Tokyo's street style is a dynamic canvas of personal expression.

Vintage Treasures: Tokyo is a goldmine for vintage fashion enthusiasts. Areas like Koenji and Shimokitazawa are renowned for their vintage shops, where you can find everything from classic American denim to rare Japanese designer pieces. It's a sustainable way to shop and a chance to own a piece of fashion history.

Fashion Events and Pop-Ups: Keep an eye out for fashion events, pop-up stores, and limited-time collaborations that frequently occur in Tokyo. These events often feature exclusive items and offer a chance to experience the cutting edge of fashion innovation up close.

Cultural Etiquette: When shopping in Tokyo, be mindful of the local customs. Many stores will package your purchases meticulously, and it's considered polite to accept the item with both hands. If you're trying on clothes, be careful to keep makeup and perfume from transferring onto the garments.

Language Barrier: While the language barrier can seem daunting, many shops in Tokyo's fashion districts have staff who speak basic English, and pictograms are often used to explain store policies. Don't hesitate to use translation apps or simple English to communicate; the warmth and hospitality of Tokyo's shopkeepers often transcend language.

Payment Practices: While international credit cards are widely accepted in Tokyo's major shopping districts, it's always a good idea to carry some cash, especially if you're exploring smaller boutiques or market stalls that might not accept cards.

TRADITIONAL SOUVENIRS

Kimono and Yukata: The kimono, with its elegant fabric and intricate designs, is a symbol of Japanese tradition. While purchasing a new kimono can be quite an investment, many shops in Tokyo offer vintage kimonos at more accessible prices. For a lighter, more casual version, the yukata provides a perfect alternative, especially in the warmer months. Shops in Asakusa and around Senso-ji temple offer a wide range of these garments, along with all the necessary accessories.

Pottery and Ceramics: Japanese pottery, with its diverse range of styles and finishes, offers a beautiful and practical souvenir option. Tokyo's Kappabashi Street, known as Kitchen Town, is lined with stores selling exquisite ceramics that range from rustic, hand-crafted mugs to sleek, modern plates. Each piece reflects the Japanese aesthetic of finding beauty in imperfection, making them unique gifts or additions to your home.

Lacquerware: Known in Japan as urushi, lacquerware is a traditional craft that produces stunningly beautiful items, from bento boxes to serving trays. The glossy finish and durability of lacquerware make it a prized possession. Shops in the Ginza district often showcase high-quality lacquerware, where the depth of the craftsmanship is on full display.

Japanese Stationery: Tokyo is a paradise for stationery enthusiasts. Japanese stationery is renowned for its quality and design, from silky-smooth writing paper to meticulously crafted pens and whimsical washi tape. Stores like Itoya in Ginza or Tokyu Hands in Shibuya offer floors upon floors of stationery goods that are both functional and beautiful, perfect for gifts or personal use.

Swords and Knives: For those interested in the martial aspect of Japanese culture, a visit to a specialist store selling samurai swords (katana) can be fascinating. While authentic swords are expensive and subject to strict export regulations, replica swords or beautifully crafted kitchen knives are excellent alternatives. Knife shops in Tsukiji offer an array of Japanese blades that are as much a work of art as they are culinary tools.

Tea and Sweets: Bringing home a taste of Japan is made easy with the country's exquisite selection of teas and sweets. Green tea, or matcha, can be found in various grades and forms, from ceremonial-grade powder to tea leaves. Pair your tea with traditional Japanese sweets (wagashi), such as mochi or dorayaki, for a complete experience. Department store food halls, known as depachika, are great places to explore the vast selection of teas and sweets available.

Tips for Souvenir Shopping in Tokyo

Authenticity Matters: When shopping for traditional souvenirs, look for shops that specialize in handmade or artisanal items. These may be slightly more expensive but offer authenticity and craftsmanship that mass-produced items cannot match.

Cultural Sensitivity: When purchasing items with cultural significance, such as Buddhist statues or Shinto amulets, be mindful of their cultural and religious meanings. These items should be treated with respect.

Bargaining: While bargaining is not common practice in Japan, some markets or outdoor stalls may welcome gentle haggling. However, in most shops, prices are fixed and should be respected.

Packaging and Transportation: Many shops offer beautiful, meticulous packaging services, perfect for gifts. For larger or more fragile items, inquire about international shipping options directly from the store to ensure your treasures make it home safely.

Tax-Free Shopping: Tourists in Japan can take advantage of tax-free shopping at many stores. Be sure to bring your passport with you to qualify for tax exemption on your purchases.

CHAPTER 4
HIDDEN TOKYO TREASURES

4.1 SECRET NEIGHBORHOODS

STROLL THROUGH TIME: YANAKA

Yanaka: A Glimpse into Old Tokyo

The Essence of Yanaka: Unlike much of Tokyo, Yanaka survived the air raids of World War II and the rapid modernization that followed, retaining an atmosphere reminiscent of the Showa era. With every step through its alleys, you're treading along paths that have witnessed the ebb and flow of time, each corner a narrative of resilience and preservation.

Yanaka Ginza: The Heartbeat of the Neighborhood: At the core of Yanaka is Yanaka Ginza, a bustling shopping street that captivates with its Showa-era charm. Here, traditional storefronts offer an array of goods from handmade crafts to local sweets, each shop telling its own story. It's a place where locals and visitors alike gather, drawn by the aroma of freshly baked senbei (rice crackers) and the warm smiles of shopkeepers.

Temples and Cherry Blossoms: Yanaka is often referred to as Yanesen, together with neighboring Nezu and Sendagi, an area known for its dense concentration of temples. The most notable among them is Tennoji, featuring a bronze Buddha statue that serenely watches over the district. In spring, Yanaka Cemetery, with its sprawling cherry trees, becomes a breathtaking spot for hanami (cherry blossom viewing), where the beauty of life and the impermanence of existence are contemplated in tandem.

Art and Craftsmanship: The winding streets of Yanaka are a haven for artists and craftsmen, with galleries and workshops dotting the area. The Yanaka Art Show, a semi-annual event, transforms the neighborhood into an open-air gallery, showcasing local talent and fostering a community of creativity.

Cafes and Eateries: Amidst its historical backdrop, Yanaka has embraced the café culture, with numerous cozy spots offering a blend of traditional Japanese and modern Western fare.

Each café, from the rustic to the retro, invites you to pause, whether for a cup of hand-drip coffee or a matcha-flavored treat, providing a tranquil respite from the urban hustle.

Tips for Exploring Yanaka

Take It Slow: Yanaka's charm is best appreciated at a leisurely pace. Allow yourself to wander without a strict itinerary, discovering hidden gardens, quaint shops, and architectural gems along the way.

Respect the Quiet: While Yanaka welcomes visitors, it remains a residential area. Be mindful of the local residents' privacy and peace, keeping noise to a minimum and respecting private property.

Camera Etiquette: Yanaka is undeniably photogenic, from its streets to its temples. However, always ask for permission before taking photos of private homes or individuals, respecting the neighborhood's tranquility.

Support Local Businesses: Purchasing from the local shops and eateries in Yanaka contributes to the preservation of its cultural heritage. Many of these businesses have been passed down through generations, and your patronage helps ensure their survival.

Cultural Workshops: Look out for workshops and experiences that allow you to dive deeper into Japanese culture, from pottery classes to traditional tea ceremonies. Participating in these activities offers a hands-on connection to the traditions that shape Yanaka.

Street Art and Murals: Keep your eyes peeled for some awesome street art that adorns the walls of Yanaka. These pieces often blend traditional Japanese themes with modern artistic expressions, making for great photo ops and a unique way to see how contemporary artists respect and reinterpret traditional Japanese culture.

Yanaka Beer Hall: For a chill spot to kick back after exploring, check out the Yanaka Beer Hall. It's a cool place that serves up local craft beers in a cozy, retro setting. It's a great way to experience the local vibe while enjoying some unique Japanese brews.

Cat Town: Yanaka is famously known as "Cat Town" for its love of cats. You'll find cat-themed shops, cafés, and even street decorations celebrating our feline friends. It's a quirky aspect of Yanaka that adds to its unique character and is a must-see for cat lovers.

Historic Homes and Architecture: As you wander through Yanaka, take time to admire the traditional architecture. Some buildings and homes have been carefully preserved or restored, offering a glimpse into Tokyo's past. It's like walking through a living museum, where each structure tells a piece of Tokyo's story.

Local Festivals: If you're in Yanaka at the right time, you might catch one of the local festivals. These events are a fantastic way to experience Japanese traditions firsthand, from street parades to traditional music and dance performances. They're vibrant, lively, and a whole lot of fun.

VINTAGE COOL: SHIMOKITAZAWA

Thrift Shopping Galore: Shimokitazawa is Tokyo's vintage clothing mecca. The neighborhood is dotted with an array of thrift shops that range from small, curated boutiques to sprawling warehouses filled with second-hand goods. Each store has its own personality, offering everything from retro kimonos to vintage band tees and designer labels at a fraction of their original price. It's a treasure trove for fashion enthusiasts looking to add unique pieces to their wardrobe without breaking the bank.

Café Culture: Amidst the shopping frenzy, Shimokitazawa's café scene offers a tranquil escape. Each café, many hidden away in unassuming alleys, boasts its unique charm. From rustic spots serving hand-drip coffee to modern spaces offering vegan treats, these cafés are perfect for people-watching or whiling away an afternoon with a good book.

Live Music and Theatrical Acts: Shimokitazawa is a hub for Tokyo's indie music scene, with numerous live houses and bars hosting up-and-coming bands and solo acts almost every night of the week. The neighborhood is also known for its small theaters, where experimental and avant-garde performances take the stage, offering a glimpse into the creative soul of Tokyo.

Foodie's Delight: Beyond its vintage and music scene, Shimokitazawa is a foodie's paradise. The neighborhood is packed with eateries ranging from cozy izakayas serving traditional Japanese fare to trendy spots offering international cuisine. It's also home to some of Tokyo's best hole-in-the-wall ramen shops and sweet crepe stands.

Street Art and Culture: Shimokitazawa's artistic flair is evident in its vibrant street art and murals, which adorn the walls of its narrow lanes. The neighborhood's creative community thrives here, with galleries and workshops showcasing local art, handmade crafts, and unique jewelry, making Shimokitazawa a haven for artists and art enthusiasts alike.

Tips for Exploring Shimokitazawa

Getting Lost is Part of the Charm: Shimokitazawa's winding streets and alleys are best explored without a strict itinerary. Allow yourself to wander and discover the hidden gems that make this neighborhood so special.

Shop Ethically: Many of Shimokitazawa's thrift stores are not only about fashion but also sustainability. Shopping here supports a culture of recycling and ethical consumption, adding an extra layer of satisfaction to your finds.

Evening Vibes: While Shimokitazawa is lively during the day, it takes on a whole new character at night. The neighborhood's bars and live houses come alive, offering a perfect opportunity to experience Tokyo's indie nightlife.

Festivals and Events: Keep an eye out for local festivals and street markets, especially during the warmer months. These events are a great way to experience the community spirit of Shimokitazawa, often featuring live music, art displays, and food stalls.

Stay Connected: Follow local Shimokitazawa pages on social media for updates on pop-up events, new store openings, and live shows. It's a great way to stay in the loop and make the most of your visit.

Here are some cool, lesser-known facts and spots that make this neighborhood a must-visit for anyone looking to experience Tokyo's indie scene:

Underground Music Joints: Shimokitazawa is packed with tiny, basement music venues that are epicenters for indie and alternative music. These spots often host impromptu gigs and open-mic nights, making them perfect for catching the next big thing in music.

Retro Game Shops: For the gamers out there, Shimokitazawa has some rad shops specializing in retro video games and consoles. It's like a time capsule where you can find gems from your childhood or discover classic games from before your time.

Fashion Forward: Beyond vintage, Shimokitazawa is also a launchpad for local designers. There are several boutiques where young Tokyo designers sell their original creations, from streetwear to more avant-garde pieces. It's a great place to find something unique and support up-and-coming talent.

Artisan Coffee Shops: Shimokitazawa's coffee scene is on another level. Some of Tokyo's best baristas set up shop here, serving up specialty brews in cozy, Instagram-worthy cafes. It's not just about the caffeine; it's about the art of coffee making.

Eco-friendly Finds: In line with its indie ethos, Shimokitazawa is home to several eco-conscious shops selling everything from organic clothing to upcycled goods. Shopping here feels good not just for your wardrobe but for the planet too.

Tiny Galleries: Scattered throughout the neighborhood are tiny art galleries and exhibition spaces, often hidden away in back alleys. These spots showcase the work of local artists and photographers, offering a peek into Tokyo's contemporary art scene.

RIVERSIDE CHILL: NAKAMEGURO

The Cherry Blossom Canopy: Come spring, Nakameguro transforms into a spectacle of pink blossoms. The cherry blossoms (sakura) along the Meguro River create a stunning canopy, under which locals and visitors alike gather to celebrate hanami, the cherry blossom viewing. Cafes and restaurants along the riverfront open their doors and windows to the breathtaking view, offering seasonal treats and a perfect spot for a leisurely day out.

Cafe Culture and Culinary Delights: Nakameguro's streets are a haven for foodies and coffee enthusiasts. The neighborhood's cafe culture is strong, with places ranging from minimalist coffee shops serving artisan brews to cozy eateries offering hearty meals. The culinary scene here is diverse, reflecting Tokyo's global palate with a distinct Nakameguro twist.

Boutique Shopping: Beyond its culinary offerings, Nakameguro is renowned for its shopping scene. Boutique stores are tucked away in its narrow lanes, offering everything from high-end fashion to handcrafted goods. It's a neighborhood where independent designers flourish, providing a shopping experience far removed from the city's bustling commercial centers.

Evening Escapes by the Riverside: As the day fades, Nakameguro's riverside comes alive in a different hue. The area is known for its chic bars and izakayas, where the night is welcomed with a mix of good food, great drinks, and even better company. It's the perfect place to unwind, as the tranquil flow of the Meguro River provides a soothing backdrop.

Art and Creativity: Nakameguro's laid-back vibe attracts a creative crowd, and this is reflected in its art scene. Small galleries and studios dot the neighborhood, offering a platform for emerging artists. The art here is as diverse as the neighborhood itself, from contemporary pieces to traditional crafts.

Exploring Nakameguro: Tips for the Traveler

Seasonal Visits: While Nakameguro is beautiful year-round, visiting during the cherry blossom season in early spring or during the autumn when the leaves change color can offer a uniquely picturesque experience. However, be prepared for crowds, especially during sakura season.

Stroll without a Plan: One of Nakameguro's greatest pleasures is found in aimlessly wandering its streets. Let curiosity be your guide as you discover hidden cafes, quaint shops, and riverside nooks.

Respect the Calm: Nakameguro's charm lies in its tranquility. While exploring, be mindful of the local residents and maintain the peace that defines the neighborhood.

Try the Local Eats: Don't miss out on the local delicacies. From the comfort of a bowl of ramen to the sophistication of a meticulously prepared kaiseki meal, Nakameguro's dining scene is a reflection of Tokyo's culinary diversity.

Capture the Moments: Nakameguro is incredibly photogenic, from the riverside views to the details of a well-curated shop window. While photography is welcomed, always be respectful of people's privacy and avoid intrusive behavior.

Nighttime Riverside Walks: For a different perspective, take a nighttime stroll along the Meguro River. The area is quieter, and the illuminated pathways offer a serene experience, perfect for reflection or a romantic walk.

4.2 GREEN ESCAPES

UENO'S OUTDOOR GALLERY

Art Museums Galore: Ueno Park is celebrated for its concentration of art museums, each offering a glimpse into different eras and styles. The Tokyo National Museum holds treasures of Japanese art and artifacts, providing insight into the country's rich history and culture. The National Museum of Western Art, designed by the renowned architect Le Corbusier, showcases masterpieces from across the globe, inviting comparisons and connections across cultures. Meanwhile, the Tokyo Metropolitan Art Museum offers contemporary exhibitions that challenge and inspire, making Ueno Park a hub for art lovers.

Nature's Masterpiece: Amidst the cultural landmarks, Ueno Park itself is a masterpiece of nature. During spring, the park is famed for its cherry blossom trees, which bloom in a spectacle of soft pink, drawing visitors for picnics under the blossoms. The Shinobazu Pond, with its lotus flowers, adds to the park's natural artistry, creating a serene landscape that contrasts with the surrounding cityscape.

Historical Sites and Hidden Gems: The park is dotted with historical sites, including the Toshogu Shrine, a lavishly decorated shrine dedicated to Tokugawa Ieyasu, and the Kiyomizu Kannon Temple, offering quiet moments of reflection. Hidden amongst the greenery are statues and sculptures, some by famous artists, others by unknown hands, making every walk through the park an opportunity for discovery.

The Ueno Zoo: Within the park's boundaries lies the Ueno Zoo, Japan's oldest zoo, home to a diverse range of animals from around the world. The panda exhibit is a highlight, drawing crowds eager to catch a glimpse of these beloved creatures. The zoo, with its commitment to conservation and education, adds another layer to Ueno Park's offering, blending the beauty of wildlife with the park's cultural tapestry.

Maximizing Your Visit to Ueno's Outdoor Gallery

Early Morning Exploration: To fully appreciate Ueno Park's beauty and avoid the crowds, consider visiting early in the morning. The soft light and quiet atmosphere make it a perfect time for photography or a peaceful stroll.

Cultural Afternoons: Dedicate your afternoons to exploring the museums. Many offer free admission days or special exhibitions, so check their schedules in advance to make the most of your visit.

Seasonal Events: Ueno Park hosts various events throughout the year, from cherry blossom festivals in spring to outdoor concerts and art installations. These events offer a unique way to experience the park's vibrant community spirit.

Picnic by the Pond: For a relaxing break, grab some snacks from nearby vendors or convenience stores and enjoy a picnic by Shinobazu Pond. It's a simple pleasure that allows you to take in the park's natural beauty.

Evening Reflections: As the day winds down, take a moment to reflect by the lotus pond or under the cherry trees. Ueno's Outdoor Gallery, with its blend of art, history, and nature, offers a profound reminder of Tokyo's multifaceted identity, where every corner holds a story, and every path leads to new discoveries.

Some cool, lesser-known aspects that make Ueno Park a must-visit:

Street Performers: On weekends, Ueno Park comes alive with street performers. From musicians to magicians, these artists add a dynamic vibe to the park's atmosphere, showcasing Tokyo's lively arts scene in the most casual way.

Peony Garden: Tucked away in Ueno Park is a stunning Peony Garden that blooms in vibrant colors, especially beautiful in spring and early summer. It's a quieter spot perfect for those looking for a peaceful retreat or a great photo op away from the usual spots.

Boat Rides on Shinobazu Pond: For a different view of the park, you can rent a swan boat or a rowboat on Shinobazu Pond. It's a fun, relaxing way to see the park from the water, especially lovely during lotus season or when the leaves change color in autumn.

Art Street: Alongside the main walking paths, there's a lesser-known "Art Street" where local artists display and sell their work. It's a great place to find unique souvenirs, from handmade jewelry to original artwork, and even chat with the artists about their work.

Cafes with a View: There are several cafes within and around Ueno Park that offer stunning views of the greenery and ponds. These spots are perfect for a restful break, where you can enjoy a cup of coffee or tea while soaking in the serene park views.

SHINJUKU'S GARDEN RETREAT

In the midst of Shinjuku's neon dazzle and skyscraper silhouette, there lies an oasis of tranquility that offers a serene counterpoint to the urban adrenaline. "Shinjuku's Garden Retreat," better known as Shinjuku Gyoen National Garden, is a sprawling haven that combines the meticulous beauty of traditional Japanese gardens with the broad, open designs of Western landscapes. This blend of styles creates a unique space that invites visitors to wander, contemplate, and reconnect with nature right in the heart of one of Tokyo's most bustling districts.

Shinjuku Gyoen: A Symphony of Nature

The Traditional Japanese Garden: As you step into Shinjuku Gyoen, the Japanese Garden, with its tranquil ponds, stone bridges, and carefully pruned bonsai trees, beckons. The garden is a masterpiece of Japanese landscape design, embodying the principles of harmony and balance. It's a place where each element, from the koi fish that glide through the water to the meticulously raked gravel, contributes to an atmosphere of peaceful contemplation.

The English Landscape Garden: In contrast to the Japanese Garden's introspective beauty, the English Landscape Garden offers sprawling lawns that invite leisurely strolls and picnics under the open sky. This part of Shinjuku Gyoen feels like a patch of countryside transported to the city, complete with seasonal flowers that bloom in a riot of colors, creating a picturesque setting for relaxation and social gatherings.

The French Formal Garden: The precision and elegance of the French Formal Garden add a touch of European flair to Shinjuku Gyoen. Symmetrical arrangements of flowers and hedges frame scenic walkways, leading visitors through a meticulously designed landscape that echoes the grandeur of French royal gardens. It's a place where the art of gardening is celebrated with a flourish, offering a visually stunning experience.

Cherry Blossom Viewing Spots: Shinjuku Gyoen is renowned for its cherry blossom spots, which draw visitors from near and far during the sakura season. With over a thousand cherry trees, the garden offers one of Tokyo's most spectacular cherry blossom displays. The variety of cherry trees ensures that blooms can be enjoyed for a longer period, from the early bloomers in March to the late-flowering varieties in April.

The Greenhouse: For those interested in botany or simply seeking a burst of greenery, Shinjuku Gyoen's greenhouse is a treasure trove of tropical and subtropical plants. The greenhouse hosts a collection of rare plant species, providing a lush, verdant escape and an opportunity to learn about diverse flora from around the world.

Navigating Shinjuku's Garden Retreat: Tips for the Explorer

Plan Your Visit: Shinjuku Gyoen has different areas that shine in various seasons. Whether it's the cherry blossoms of spring, the fiery maples of autumn, or the lush greenery of summer, planning your visit based on what you wish to see can enhance your experience.

Mind the Opening Hours: Unlike some public parks, Shinjuku Gyoen has set opening hours and a small entrance fee. Check the current hours and fees before your visit to ensure you make the most of your time in the garden.

Picnic with Respect: While picnicking is allowed, it's important to do so with respect for the garden and other visitors. Use the designated areas, dispose of your trash properly, and keep the noise to a minimum to preserve the peaceful atmosphere.

Photography Etiquette: Shinjuku Gyoen is a photographer's dream, but remember to be courteous when taking photos, especially during the busy cherry blossom season. Avoid blocking pathways and respect areas where photography may be restricted.

Discover Quiet Corners: Despite its popularity, Shinjuku Gyoen is vast enough to offer quiet corners and hidden spots away from the crowds. Take the path less traveled to discover your own peaceful retreat within the garden.

MOUNTAIN DAY TRIP: TAKAO

Just a short train ride away from the neon lights and bustling streets of Tokyo lies Mount Takao, a natural sanctuary that offers city dwellers and travelers alike a breath of fresh air and a chance to immerse themselves in the beauty of Japan's landscapes. "Mountain Day Trip: Takao" is not just about escaping the city's fast pace; it's about connecting with nature, exploring ancient trails, and experiencing the spiritual heritage that makes this mountain a revered site.

Embracing Nature at Mount Takao

The Trails: Mount Takao boasts several trails that cater to all levels of hikers, from the leisurely stroll of Trail 1, which is paved and accessible, to the more adventurous paths like Trail 6, which takes you through the mountain's untouched natural beauty. Each trail offers its unique vistas, from cascading waterfalls to panoramic views of Tokyo and, on clear days, the majestic Mount Fuji on the horizon.

Cultural and Spiritual Sites: Along the trails, you'll encounter various cultural and spiritual sites that add depth to your hike. The Yakuoin Temple is a highlight, a place of worship nestled among the trees where you can learn about the mountain's spiritual significance and even partake in Buddhist rituals. Statues of Tengu, mythical creatures revered as protectors of the mountains, can be found along the paths, adding a mystical element to your journey.

Seasonal Splendors: Each season brings a new reason to visit Mount Takao. Spring welcomes cherry blossoms and vibrant azaleas, summer is lush and green, autumn adorns the mountain in fiery foliage, and winter, though more subdued, offers clear, crisp air and the chance for snow-capped views. The changing seasons ensure that no two visits to Mount Takao are ever the same.

Culinary Delights: Hiking works up an appetite, and Mount Takao doesn't disappoint. Near the summit and at the base, local eateries offer treats like tororo soba (noodles with grated yam) and dango (rice dumplings), providing a taste of the local cuisine. For a unique experience, try the tofu made with the mountain's natural spring water.

The Cable Car and Chair Lift: For those who wish to save their energy or simply enjoy the ride, a cable car and a chair lift offer alternatives to hiking to the summit. Both provide scenic views of the surrounding nature and are an experience in their own right.

Tips for Your Takao Adventure

Start Early: To make the most of your day trip and avoid the crowds, especially during peak seasons, start your hike early in the morning. This also increases your chances of catching the best views before any afternoon clouds roll in.

Preparation is Key: Wear comfortable hiking shoes and bring layers, as the weather can change quickly in the mountains. Don't forget water and snacks, although there are vending machines and shops along the way for refreshments.

Respect Nature: Stay on the paths, dispose of trash properly, and keep noise to a minimum to preserve the tranquility and natural beauty of Mount Takao.

Explore the Surrounding Area: The area around Mount Takao, including the Keio Takaosan Onsen Gokurakuyu near the base, offers a chance to soak in hot springs after your hike, adding a relaxing end to your adventure.

Capture the Moment: Bring a camera or make sure your phone is charged. The views from Mount Takao, the cultural sites, and even the flora and fauna you'll encounter are worth capturing and sharing.

Some pretty cool, less talked-about opportunities for anyone ready to explore a bit more:

Fire Walking Festival: If you're into seeing something unique, check out the Hiwatari Matsuri (Fire Walking Festival) at Yakuoin Temple. Monks walk across burning coals and then open it to the public to try. It's said to cleanse and purify one's soul.

Monkey Park: Yes, there's a spot where you can see monkeys up close! Near the halfway point of the mountain, there's a monkey park where you can learn about and observe Japanese macaques in their natural habitat. It's a fun break from hiking and a hit if you're into wildlife.

Beer Garden: During the summer months, there's a beer garden at the summit. Imagine chilling with a cold drink after a hike, soaking in the views. It's a vibe that combines relaxation with a sense of achievement.

Night Hiking: For the adventurous souls, night hiking on Mount Takao offers a different perspective. The trails are quiet, and reaching the summit in time to catch the sunrise is an unforgettable experience. Just make sure to go in a group and take the necessary safety precautions.

Takaosan Tricking Hall: If you're into learning about illusions and trick art, this place is a quirky museum where you can check out optical illusions and trick art, making for some fun photo ops and a break from the usual cultural spots.

4.3 QUIRKY CORNERS

CAFÉS: CATS, OWLS, AND ROBOTS

The Purrfect Escape: Cat Cafés

The concept of cat cafés has evolved into an art form. These cozy spots offer refuge not just for humans looking for a place to relax but also for felines that have found a permanent home among couches and coffee tables. Cat cafés in Tokyo vary from the homey to the sophisticated, with each establishment boasting its unique ambiance and a variety of cat breeds to meet. It's a place where you can enjoy a warm drink while a furry friend curls up in your lap—a simple joy for animal lovers and a soothing escape from the urban hustle.

A Hoot of a Time: Owl Cafés

Owl cafés offer an entirely different experience. These establishments allow visitors to get up close and personal with owls of various species, from the tiny to the majestic. It's an intimate encounter with these nocturnal birds, often accompanied by a café staff who educates visitors on owl behavior and conservation efforts. While the concept might seem outlandish, it's a testament to Tokyo's love for themed experiences and the city's ability to turn even a café visit into an adventure.

The Future Is Now: Robot Cafés

Stepping into a robot café is like walking into a sci-fi movie set in motion. These high-tech spots offer a glimpse into the future, where robots serve drinks, prepare meals, and even put on performances. The Robot Restaurant in Shinjuku, for example, is less about the food and more about the spectacle—a dazzling show of lights, robots, and music that captivates and entertains. It's a uniquely Tokyo experience that combines technology, art, and dining in a way that can only be described as electric.

Tips for Enjoying Tokyo's Quirkiest Cafés

Reservations Recommended: These unique cafés are often small and can get quite busy, especially on weekends. Making a reservation can ensure you get a spot, particularly at the more popular locations.

Mind the Rules: Each café, especially animal cafés, has its own set of rules to ensure the safety and well-being of the animals and visitors. Pay attention to these guidelines to make the experience enjoyable for everyone involved.

Embrace the Experience: Whether it's interacting with cats, marveling at owls, or being entertained by robots, each café offers more than just food and drinks—it offers stories to share and memories to cherish.

Sustainability and Ethics: When visiting animal cafés, consider the welfare of the animals. Look for establishments that prioritize the health and happiness of their animals, providing them with ample space, rest periods, and proper care.

Capture the Moment, Respectfully: While photos are encouraged, remember to use your camera respectfully, especially in animal cafés. Avoid flash photography that can startle the animals, and always prioritize their comfort over the perfect shot.

Book and Literary Cafés

For those who find solace in the pages of a book, Tokyo's literary cafés are a haven. Imagine sipping on a latte surrounded by floor-to-ceiling bookshelves, with the soft rustle of pages turning in the background. These cafés often host readings, book launches, and informal discussions, making them a hotspot for bibliophiles and writers alike. Some even offer the chance to curl up with a book in cozy nooks, blurring the line between café and library.

Gaming and E-Sports Cafés

Gaming enthusiasts will find their paradise in Tokyo's gaming and e-sports cafés. Equipped with high-end PCs, consoles, and VR setups, these cafés offer an array of games to choose from, whether you're into the latest RPGs, classic arcade games, or competitive e-sports. The atmosphere is electric, with live streams of tournaments, themed drinks, and a community of fellow gamers to share in the excitement.

Art and Craft Cafés

For the creatively inclined, art and craft cafés provide a space to unleash your artistic side. These establishments supply the materials—be it canvas, pottery, or fabric—and you bring the inspiration. It's a relaxing way to spend an afternoon, creating something unique while enjoying your favorite drink. Workshops led by local artists are also common, offering guided experiences in everything from painting to knitting.

Nature and Garden Cafés

These spaces are designed with an emphasis on greenery, featuring indoor gardens, vertical plant walls, and even small streams running through the café. The connection to nature extends to the menu, with organic, locally sourced ingredients taking center stage. It's a serene escape for those looking to recharge among lush foliage and natural light.

Pop Culture and Fan Cafés

Dedicated to various facets of pop culture, these cafés cater to fans of specific anime, manga, movie, or music band. Decorated in memorabilia and offering themed dishes, these spots provide a place for fans to celebrate their passions. Special events, like anniversary celebrations of popular series or album launches, turn these cafés into buzzing hubs of excitement and fandom.

Tips for Café Hopping in Tokyo

Language Tips: While some café staff may speak English, having a translation app or a phrasebook can help smooth over any language barriers, especially in more niche spots.

Cultural Sensitivity: Remember, each themed café is a world of its own, with its rules and etiquette. Always be respectful of the theme and the other patrons who are there to enjoy the immersive experience.

Explore Off the Beaten Path: While the well-known themed cafés are worth a visit, don't be afraid to explore smaller, lesser-known spots. These hidden gems often offer the most authentic and memorable experiences.

Mind the Time: Some popular cafés can have long wait times, especially on weekends or holidays. Plan accordingly, and consider visiting during off-peak hours for a more relaxed experience.

Souvenirs and Merchandise: Many themed cafés offer exclusive merchandise, making for unique souvenirs that you can't find anywhere else. Keep an eye out for these special items to take a piece of the experience home with you.

Cafés

A Sanctuary in the City: For many Tokyo residents and visitors, cat cafés offer a peaceful escape from the hustle and bustle of city life. These spaces provide a unique opportunity to unwind and interact with cats, each with its own personality, in a cozy setting. It's not just about petting cats; it's about the therapeutic effect they have on people, offering comfort and a sense of calm.

The Cats: Each cat café in Tokyo tends to house a variety of breeds, from the sleek and elegant Siamese to the fluffy majesty of the Maine Coon. Some cafés even focus on rescues and mixed breeds, giving them a loving home and a second chance. The well-being of the cats is paramount, with many cafés implementing strict rules to ensure their health and happiness. Visitors get to learn about each cat's backstory, making the connection even more special.

More Than Just Coffee: While the presence of cats is the main draw, these cafés often go beyond serving drinks. They create a community space where cat lovers can come together, share stories, and participate in events like cat-themed art workshops or talks on feline care. The café environment encourages social interaction not just with the cats but among the visitors themselves, fostering a sense of community.

Innovative Experiences: Some cat cafés in Tokyo offer unique experiences that set them apart. For instance, there are cafés that feature rare and exotic breeds, giving visitors the chance to meet cats they might not otherwise encounter. Others might combine the café concept with a bookstore or art gallery, creating a multifaceted cultural experience centered around the love for cats.

Navigating Tokyo's Cat Cafés

Respect the Residents: The cats are not just attractions; they're the beloved inhabitants of the cafés. It's important to follow the rules regarding handling and interacting with them—usually, gentle petting is welcome, but picking them up or disturbing their sleep is not.

Contribution to Animal Welfare: Many cat cafés in Tokyo play an active role in promoting animal welfare, with some of the entrance fees going towards cat rescue organizations or covering the care of stray and abandoned cats. By visiting these cafés, patrons indirectly contribute to these causes.

Hygiene and Comfort: Cat cafés maintain high standards of cleanliness for the comfort of both the cats and the visitors. Upon entering, you'll often be asked to remove your shoes and sanitize your hands, ensuring a clean environment for everyone.

Making the Most of Your Visit: To truly enjoy the cat café experience, it's best to go without expectations. Cats have their own wills and personalities; some may seek out your attention, while others may prefer to observe from afar. The beauty of these cafés lies in their unpredictability and the natural behavior of the cats.

Finding Your Perfect Match: With the variety of cat cafés available in Tokyo, it's worth exploring a few to find the one that best matches your vibe. Whether you're looking for a quiet place to read and relax with a cat by your side or a lively spot to meet fellow cat enthusiasts, there's a cat café in Tokyo that's perfect for you.

Owl:

A Glimpse into the Avian World: Owl cafés house a variety of owl species, from the tiny and adorable to the large and majestic. Visitors have the chance to see these birds up close, observe their behaviors, and even gently pet them under the supervision of knowledgeable staff. It's an educational experience as much as it is an enjoyable one, providing insights into the lives of owls and their significance in various cultures.

Caring and Ethical Considerations: The best owl cafés in Tokyo prioritize the welfare of their feathered residents. They ensure the owls have ample space, regular breaks, and proper care. These establishments often take the time to educate visitors about owl conservation and the natural habitats of these birds, fostering a deeper appreciation and respect for wildlife.

A Moment of Connection: For many, the appeal of owl cafés lies in the unique interaction with these birds. Owls, with their serene demeanor and deep, captivating eyes, have a way of calming the mind. The experience of having an owl perch on your arm, looking at you curiously, creates a moment of connection that's both exhilarating and soothing.

Photography with Respect: Owl cafés offer fantastic opportunities for photography, allowing visitors to capture the beauty of these creatures in a controlled setting. However, it's important to use cameras without flash and to follow the café's guidelines to ensure the owls are not disturbed by the process.

Tips for Visiting Owl Cafés

Booking in Advance: Owl cafés are quite popular, and space is often limited to ensure the comfort of the owls. It's advisable to book your visit in advance, especially if you're planning to go during peak hours or on weekends.

Understanding the Rules: Each owl café has its own set of rules regarding how to interact with the owls, including how to touch them and how to behave inside the café. Paying close attention to these guidelines ensures a positive experience for both the visitors and the owls.

Health and Safety: The well-being of the owls and visitors is paramount. Sanitizing hands before and after interacting with the birds, and wearing protective gloves if required, are common practices in owl cafés.

Quiet and Calm: Owls are naturally calm and quiet creatures, and the atmosphere in owl cafés reflects this. Visitors are encouraged to speak softly and move slowly to maintain a peaceful environment.

Supporting Ethical Establishments: Choose owl cafés that are transparent about their care practices and actively contribute to owl conservation efforts. Supporting these establishments ensures that your visit has a positive impact.

Engaging with Robot Staff

Ordering from Robots: In robot cafés and bars, guests often order food and drinks via touchscreen menus or tablets. Robot staff then prepare and deliver the orders. This interaction is not only efficient but also adds a novel twist to the dining experience.

Interactive Performances: Some robot cafés incorporate interactive elements, where guests can control certain robots or engage in games and activities led by robotic hosts. These interactions highlight the playful side of technology, inviting guests to be part of the entertainment.

Tips for Visiting Robot-Themed Venues

Book Ahead: The Robot Restaurant and other popular robot-themed venues can get fully booked, especially during tourist season. It's wise to reserve your spot in advance to avoid missing out on this unique experience.

Set Expectations: While the focus at these venues is on entertainment and technology, the culinary offerings might be secondary. Enjoy the food, but come for the robots and the spectacle.

Photography and Video: These venues are a visual feast, and you'll likely want to capture the memories. Check the venue's photography policy in advance; while photos and videos are usually encouraged, there may be restrictions during certain performances.

Embrace the Experience: Tokyo's robot cafés and restaurants are all about embracing the unusual and the futuristic. Dive into the experience with an open mind and a sense of adventure.

Consider the Audience: Some robot entertainment venues, like the Robot Restaurant, are geared more towards adults and might not be suitable for young children due to the loud noises and flashy lights. Check in advance if you're planning a family visit.

TOKYO FROM THE WATER

Exploring Tokyo's Waterways

Sumida River Cruises: The Sumida River is the artery through which the heart of Tokyo beats, and cruising this river provides spectacular views of the city's iconic landmarks. From the futuristic design of the Asahi Beer Hall to the historic beauty of the Senso-ji Temple, seen from the riverbank, these cruises encapsulate the essence of Tokyo's blend of the old and new. As the boat passes beneath the numerous bridges, each with its own story, you're treated to a panorama of Tokyo's evolving skyline.

Tokyo Bay Excursions: To see Tokyo's futuristic architecture in full splendor, a boat trip around Tokyo Bay is unmatched. The Rainbow Bridge, with its multicolored lights, creates a stunning gateway to Odaiba, a man-made island known for its entertainment complexes and shopping districts. From the water, the juxtaposition of the tranquil bay against the backdrop of Tokyo's bustling metropolis offers a moment of reflection on the city's dynamic growth and its harmonious relationship with the sea.

Historic Canal Routes: The lesser-known canals of Tokyo, remnants of a bygone era, provide a glimpse into the city's past. The Nihonbashi and Kanda rivers are lined with warehouses and traditional shops that harken back to Tokyo's days as Edo, the nation's pre-modern capital. A leisurely kayak tour through these waterways reveals hidden gems of architecture and pockets of tranquility amidst the urban expanse.

Riverbank Dining and Festivals: Tokyo's riverside is a stage for seasonal festivities and culinary delights. The cherry blossom season transforms the banks of the Sumida River into a lively picnic spot, while summer brings fireworks that light up the night sky, reflected in the water below. Along these banks, riverside cafés and restaurants serve up dishes that are best enjoyed with a view of the water, offering a dining experience that's uniquely Tokyo.

Tips for Enjoying Tokyo's Waterways

Choose Your Experience: From leisurely dinner cruises to active kayaking adventures, Tokyo's waterways offer a variety of experiences. Consider what suits your interests and energy levels best to fully enjoy the journey.

Seasonal Sensations: While Tokyo's rivers and bays are beautiful year-round, each season offers something special. Spring and autumn are particularlypicturesque, with cherry blossoms and autumn leaves adding a splash of color to the riverbanks.

Nighttime Views: For a different vibe, consider taking a boat cruise after dark. Tokyo's skyline is dramatically lit at night, and viewing it from the water adds an extra layer of magic to the experience.

Respect the Water: If you opt for a more hands-on experience like kayaking, be mindful of water safety. Follow the guidelines provided by tour operators and respect the natural environment to ensure a safe and enjoyable trip.

Capture the Moment: Don't forget your camera. Whether it's the architectural marvels, the serene landscapes, or the unique perspective of the city, there's no shortage of photo opportunities when exploring Tokyo from the water.

MAKE YOUR OWN SOUVENIR

Crafting Memories in Tokyo

Pottery Workshops in Kichijoji: Venture into the charming neighborhood of Kichijoji, where pottery studios offer workshops for beginners and experienced potters alike. Under the guidance of local artisans, mold, glaze, and fire your own piece of pottery. Whether it's a delicate tea cup or a rustic bowl, the experience of shaping clay on a potter's wheel connects you to an art form that has been part of Japanese culture for centuries.

Indigo Dyeing in Shibuya: Shibuya, known for its bustling streets and fashion-forward spirit, is also home to workshops specializing in indigo dyeing. Learn the traditional Japanese technique of Shibori, where cloth is twisted, bound, folded, and dyed to create intricate patterns. The rich, vibrant blue of indigo not only makes for a beautiful fabric but also tells a story of Japan's long-standing relationship with this natural dye.

Woodblock Printing in Asakusa: Asakusa, with its historic sensibilities, offers the chance to delve into the world of Ukiyo-e, the art of woodblock printing. Join a workshop where you're taken through the process of carving your design into wood, inking the block, and then pressing it onto paper to create your own print. This art form, which flourished during the Edo period, allows you to connect with Tokyo's artistic heritage while creating a unique piece of art.

Calligraphy Classes: The art of Japanese calligraphy, or Shodo, is a practice of precision, mindfulness, and expression. Across Tokyo, from traditional teahouses to contemporary art spaces, calligraphy workshops invite you to learn the basics of this beautiful form of writing. Armed with a brush and ink, learn how to write your name or a favorite word in Japanese characters, creating a deeply personal souvenir.

Tips for a Fulfilling DIY Experience

Book in Advance: Many workshops require booking in advance, especially those with limited space or popular ones led by renowned artisans. Planning ahead ensures you secure a spot in the workshop of your choice.

Embrace the Process: Creating your own souvenir is as much about the experience and the memories as it is about the final product. Embrace each step of the process, from the initial learning curve to the final creation.

Respect the Craft: Participating in these workshops offers a glimpse into the dedication and skill behind traditional and contemporary Japanese crafts. Approach each workshop with respect for the art form and its cultural significance.

Ask Questions: Engaging with the artisans and instructors not only enriches your understanding of the craft but also deepens your connection to the culture. Don't hesitate to ask questions about the history, techniques, and personal stories behind their work.

Share Your Experience: Your DIY souvenir is a story in itself, a tangible memory of your time in Tokyo. Share the story of its creation with friends and family—it adds value and depth to the souvenir, making it a cherished item for years to come.

4.4 ROAD TRIPS

HOT SPRINGS AND FUJI VIEWS

The Majestic Mount Fuji

Mount Fuji, Japan's iconic symbol, offers more than just a stunning backdrop for photos. The areas surrounding this majestic peak are filled with opportunities for adventure, cultural experiences, and moments of awe. Whether you're admiring Fuji from a distance or exploring its slopes, the mountain has a way of captivating the heart and soul.

Fuji Five Lakes: The Fuji Five Lakes (Fujigoko) area is a perfect starting point for your road trip. Each lake offers a unique view of Mount Fuji, with opportunities for boating, camping, and leisurely walks along the shorelines. The changing seasons bring new perspectives of beauty, from cherry blossoms in spring to rich autumn colors.

Climbing Mount Fuji: For the adventurous, climbing Mount Fuji during the official climbing season (July to early September) is a once-in-a-lifetime experience. The overnight trek to watch the sunrise from the summit is challenging but rewarding, with each step bringing a new view and a deeper connection to this sacred mountain.

Onsen: Japan's Hot Spring Heaven

No road trip in the Fuji region is complete without a visit to an onsen. These natural hot springs are not just about relaxation; they're about experiencing a cherished Japanese tradition that rejuvenates the body and mind.

Hakone: Just a short drive from Tokyo, Hakone is renowned for its onsen resorts set amidst mountains and serene nature. Here, you can soak in mineral-rich waters while enjoying views of lush forests and, on clear days, Mount Fuji itself. Hakone also offers art museums, a historic checkpoint, and the Hakone Shrine, making it a rich cultural experience.

Izu Peninsula: Further down the coast, the Izu Peninsula offers onsen experiences with a sea view. The coastline is dotted with onsen towns like Atami and Ito, where you can enjoy the therapeutic benefits of hot springs while listening to the soothing sounds of the ocean.

Tips for a Fulfilling Road Trip

Plan Your Route: While the focus might be on Mount Fuji and onsen, the journey itself offers hidden gems. Plan your route to include local villages, scenic viewpoints, and culinary stops.

Respect Onsen Etiquette: Onsen have specific customs, from washing before entering the baths to keeping voices low. Familiarize yourself with these practices to ensure a respectful and enjoyable experience for everyone.

Weather Considerations: The weather can greatly affect your view of Mount Fuji. Early mornings and late afternoons tend to offer clearer views, but always have a backup plan in case the weather doesn't cooperate. **Stay Overnight:** To fully experience the onsen and have the best chance of seeing Mount Fuji without the clouds, consider staying overnight at a ryokan (traditional Japanese inn). These accommodations often offer kaiseki meals (multi-course dinners) and private onsen baths.

Pack Appropriately: For those planning to climb Mount Fuji or explore the outdoors, proper gear is essential. Even in summer, temperatures at the summit can be freezing. For onsen visits, most facilities provide everything you need, but a small towel and toiletries can come in handy.

There are hidden gems and insider tips that can make your road trip even cooler and more memorable:

Secret Spots for Fuji Views: Aside from the popular viewing spots, there are lesser-known locations where you can catch breathtaking views of Mount Fuji without the crowds. For example, the Chureito Pagoda offers a stunning backdrop of Fuji, especially during cherry blossom season or autumn. Finding these spots usually requires a bit of research or chatting with locals, but it's totally worth it for that perfect, crowd-free photo.

Nighttime Onsen Experience: Imagine soaking in a hot spring under the stars, with the night sounds of nature around you. Some onsen offer nighttime baths, which can be a magical experience, especially if you're staying in an area with minimal light pollution. It's a different vibe from the daytime and feels super exclusive.

Local Eats and Treats: The areas around Mount Fuji and onsen towns are known for more than just scenery; they have some killer local cuisine. Look out for specialty dishes like Yamanashi's houtou noodles, a hearty, miso-based stew with thick noodles and vegetables, perfect after a chilly day exploring. Local markets and roadside stands also offer fresh, seasonal fruits like peaches and grapes that are out of this world.

Cycling Routes: For a bit of adventure, consider renting a bicycle and exploring the area on two wheels. The Fuji Five Lakes area, in particular, has some scenic cycling routes that offer a fresh perspective of the landscape and Mount Fuji. It's an eco-friendly way to explore, and you get to cover more ground than on foot.

Cultural Festivals: Depending on when you visit, you might catch one of the local festivals or events that offer a deep dive into Japanese culture. From fireworks festivals in summer to the Fuji Shibazakura Festival in spring, where pink moss phlox blooms create a vibrant carpet at the foot of Mount Fuji, these events are a fantastic way to experience local traditions and community spirit.

SEASIDE STATUES: KAMAKURA

At the heart of Kamakura's spiritual landscape stands the Great Buddha (Daibutsu), a bronze statue of Amida Buddha that invites awe and reflection. Seated in the open air, this monumental figure has weathered centuries, embodying the impermanence and resilience preached in Buddhist teachings. Visiting the Great Buddha, one can't help but feel a connection to the past, a moment of stillness in the midst of life's storms. It's an encounter that goes beyond sightseeing; it's a dialogue with history.

Hasedera Temple: A View to the Sea

A short walk from the Great Buddha, Hasedera Temple offers a different kind of serenity. Known for its wooden statue of Kannon, the temple is set on a hillside, with gardens that bloom in a riot of colors through the seasons. The real surprise, however, is the view from the top. Overlooking the town and the sea beyond, Hasedera’s viewing platform offers a moment of contemplation, where the spiritual and the scenic merge into one breathtaking panorama.

Engakuji Temple: Among the Zen

Kamakura’s Zen temples offer a glimpse into the practice and philosophy that shaped Japan's medieval era. Engakuji, one of the most important Zen temples, stands as a testament to the simplicity and depth of Zen Buddhism. Walking through its grounds, among ancient trees and understated architecture, visitors are invited to experience Zen’s focus on the present moment, perhaps catching a glimpse of the monks in meditation or the sound of bamboo swaying gently in the breeze.

The Beach: A Seaside Retreat

Kamakura’s beaches are a chapter on their own. In summer, they come alive with surfers and families enjoying the sun. But the off-season brings its own charm—a quiet, expansive view of the sea, often with Mount Fuji visible in the distance. It’s a place to breathe deeply, to let the ocean’s rhythm sync with your own, and to find peace in the vastness.

Tips for the Road Trip to Kamakura

Early Start: Beat the crowds and start your day early. The tranquility of Kamakura’s sites is best enjoyed in the morning calm.

Cultural Etiquette: When visiting temples, remember to respect the customs. Quiet voices, removed shoes, and no photos in certain areas are common rules.

Local Delicacies: Kamakura is known for its sweet potatoes, among other local specialties. Don’t miss trying some of the local treats available at street vendors or cafes.

Walking Paths: Much of Kamakura’s beauty can be found in wandering its streets and trails. The Daibutsu Hiking Course, for example, offers a scenic route between the Great Buddha and Hasedera.

Travel Off-Peak: To fully appreciate Kamakura's serene beauty, consider visiting during the week when the town is less crowded.

Hidden Cafés: Tucked away in Kamakura's side streets are some chill cafés that serve up not just great coffee and snacks, but also vibes that you won't find anywhere else. Picture sipping a matcha latte in a traditional Japanese house turned café, overlooking a Zen garden.

Local Craft Shops: Kamakura has a bunch of small shops selling handmade crafts, from pottery to jewelry inspired by traditional Japanese designs. These places are perfect for picking up unique souvenirs that aren't just the usual tourist stuff.

Beachside Hangouts: While the main beaches get packed, there are smaller, quieter spots along the coast where you can hang out, enjoy the sea breeze, and maybe even catch a local band playing.

Bamboo Groves: Away from the main temples, there are bamboo groves that feel like you've stepped into another world. It's super peaceful, and the light filtering through the bamboo is perfect for that Insta-worthy shot.

Cool Festivals: Depending on when you visit, you might catch one of Kamakura's local festivals. They're a fun way to see traditional Japanese culture up close, from parades to music and dance performances.

4.5 SEASONAL CELEBRATIONS

CHERRY BLOSSOM VIEWING

As winter's chill recedes, Tokyo's landscape undergoes a mesmerizing change. Parks, riversides, and even streets become canvases for nature's delicate artistry, painted with the soft pinks and whites of cherry blossoms. This period, typically spanning from late March to early April, sees the city at its most picturesque, with locals and visitors alike pausing to admire the ephemeral beauty of sakura.

Hanami: More Than Just Flower Viewing

The practice of hanami, or cherry blossom viewing, is a deeply ingrained cultural tradition that goes beyond simply looking at flowers. It's a celebration of life, a gathering of friends and family, and a moment to reflect on the transient nature of existence. Picnics under the blossoming trees, accompanied by food, drinks, and laughter, are common, turning Tokyo's green spaces into lively communal halls.

Best Spots for Cherry Blossom Viewing

Ueno Park: One of Tokyo's most popular hanami destinations, Ueno Park boasts over a thousand cherry trees. The festive atmosphere here is unmatched, with food stalls and entertainers adding to the vibrant scene.

Chidorigafuchi: For a more serene experience, the moat surrounding the Imperial Palace, known as Chidorigafuchi, offers boat rentals for a unique view of cherry blossoms from the water.

Shinjuku Gyoen: Offering a variety of cherry tree species, Shinjuku Gyoen is perfect for those who wish to enjoy sakura in a more tranquil setting. The garden's spacious lawns are ideal for a leisurely picnic away from the crowds.

Meguro River: The banks of the Meguro River become a stunning tunnel of blossoms, creating a picturesque path for leisurely strolls. The lanterns lit up at night add a magical touch to the already breathtaking scenery.

Tips for Enjoying Cherry Blossom Season

Timing is Everything: The cherry blossom season is brief, and full bloom (mankai) lasts only a few days. Keep an eye on cherry blossom forecasts to plan your visit accordingly.

Respect the Space: Hanami is a communal experience, but it's important to respect public spaces. Clean up after your picnic, and avoid picking blossoms or branches.

Explore Beyond the Popular: While famous spots have their charm, Tokyo is dotted with lesser-known parks and streets that offer equally beautiful cherry blossom views without the crowds. Venture into residential areas or follow a local's recommendation to discover these hidden gems.

Nighttime Views (Yozakura): Many cherry blossom spots are illuminated at night, offering a different but equally enchanting experience. The blossoms under the glow of lanterns create a romantic and surreal atmosphere.

Cultural Events: Sakura season is also marked by numerous cultural events and festivals. From traditional tea ceremonies under the blossoms to sakura-themed exhibitions, these events offer a deeper dive into Japan's rich cultural tapestry.

There's a bunch of cool, less talked-about stuff that can make your sakura experience even more epic:

Local Snacks: During cherry blossom season, lots of places start selling limited-time sakura-themed snacks and drinks. Imagine pink mochi, sakura-flavored lattes, and even cherry blossom ice cream. These treats are not just Instagram-worthy; they're super tasty and totally capture the vibe of the season.

Sakura at Night: Known as "yozakura," cherry blossoms at night are a whole different scene. Some parks set up lanterns or lights that illuminate the blossoms, creating this magical, almost dreamy atmosphere. It's way less crowded, and the vibes are just perfect for chilling with friends or a special someone.

Photography Tips: Wanna snap some killer photos? Look for spots where you can get cherry blossoms in the foreground with iconic Tokyo landmarks in the back. Early morning or late afternoon is the best time for that soft, natural light that makes the blossoms pop.

Secret Spots: Sure, the big parks are cool, but Tokyo is full of hidden spots where you can enjoy the cherry blossoms away from the crowds. Small neighborhood parks, temple grounds, or even along quieter stretches of river can offer some of the best, most chill sakura viewing opportunities.

Festivals and Markets: Keep an eye out for local sakura festivals and markets. They're not just about the flowers; they often feature live music, art, and tons of street food. It's a great way to experience the local culture and see how Tokyoites celebrate the season.

SUMMER LIGHTS AND DANCES

Tokyo kicks off its summer festivities with Tanabata, celebrated in early July. Based on a romantic legend, it's a day when two star-crossed lovers, represented by stars Vega and Altair, are said to meet across the Milky Way. Streets and shopping arcades are adorned with bamboo branches, where people hang tanzaku (small pieces of paper) with their wishes written on them. Walking through these colorful displays, one can't help but feel a part of Tokyo's communal hopes and dreams.

Firework Festivals: A Symphony of Light

No summer in Tokyo is complete without its grand firework festivals, known as "Hanabi Taikai." These festivals light up the night sky with breathtaking displays, drawing crowds who gather along riversides and in parks, often dressed in traditional yukata, to enjoy the spectacle. The Sumida River Firework Festival is one of the oldest and most famous, where the sky above the river becomes a canvas for a dazzling array of fireworks. It's a celebration where the excitement is palpable, and the collective awe under the night sky unites everyone in attendance.

Bon Odori: The Dance of Ancestors

Bon Odori, the traditional dance festival, is a heartfelt tribute to the spirits of ancestors, celebrated across Tokyo in various localities during the summer months. Each region has its unique dance style and music, but the essence remains the same: a joyous celebration of life, remembrance, and community. Joining in the circular dance around a yagura (tower) to the beat of taiko drums is an immersive way to experience the warmth and inclusivity of Tokyo's local communities.

Mitama Matsuri: The Festival of Souls

Yasukuni Shrine's Mitama Matsuri, held in mid-July, is one of Tokyo's most visually stunning events. The shrine's approach is illuminated by thousands of lanterns, creating a serene path that invites reflection and remembrance. The festival also includes concerts, traditional performances, and stalls selling summer treats, blending solemnity with celebration in a uniquely Tokyo way.

Tips for Enjoying Tokyo's Summer Festivals

Stay Hydrated: Tokyo's summer can be hot and humid. When attending outdoor festivals, always carry water to stay hydrated.

Respect Cultural Practices: While joining in the festivities, be mindful of local customs and practices, especially at religious or traditional events.

Dress Appropriately: Embrace the spirit of the festivals by wearing a yukata. Many shops offer rentals and dressing services, making it easy for everyone to partake in this traditional summer wear.

Check Dates and Locations: Summer festivals happen throughout Tokyo, often on specific dates. Planning ahead ensures you won't miss out on these seasonal highlights.

Be Prepared for Crowds: Popular festivals can get crowded. Arrive early to secure a good spot, especially for firework festivals, and be patient and respectful of fellow festival-goers.

Experiences that might not make the usual travel guides but are totally worth checking out:

Urban Beaches: Tokyo sets up several "urban beaches" in the summer where you can chill, play volleyball, or just soak up the sun without leaving the city. It's like a mini-vacation spot right in the middle of the urban hustle.

Night Pools: Many hotels and venues open up their pools for nighttime parties during the summer. These are not just for swimming; they're full-on events with DJs, drinks, and sometimes even light shows. It's a cool way to beat the heat and experience Tokyo's nightlife in a different setting.

Rooftop Beer Gardens: Taking advantage of Tokyo's skyscrapers, rooftop beer gardens become popular in the summer. It's a great spot to enjoy the evening breeze, hang out with friends, and try out a variety of beers and barbecues. The view of the city skyline is a bonus.

Summer Sonic: For music lovers, the Summer Sonic festival brings in big international and local acts for a weekend of music in August. It's a blast to see your favorite bands and discover new ones in the energetic atmosphere of a music fest.

Morning Markets: Early risers can check out the morning markets that pop up in various neighborhoods during the summer. They're a great place to grab fresh, local produce, handmade crafts, and try some street food breakfast.

AUTUMN LEAVES AND WINTER SPARKLES

As the air cools and the days shorten, Tokyo's green spaces begin their spectacular transition. The city's parks, gardens, and even street-lined ginkgo trees don a vibrant array of reds, oranges, and yellows. This natural phenomenon, known as "koyo," turns ordinary walks into mesmerizing experiences.

Meiji Jingu Gaien: One of the best spots to witness this change is at Meiji Jingu Gaien, where the golden ginkgo trees create a breathtaking corridor of color. It's a favorite among both locals and visitors for leisurely strolls and photography.

Rikugien Garden: For a more traditional experience, Rikugien Garden offers a stunning display of autumn colors, especially during its evening illumination events. The meticulously maintained landscape garden, with its pond, hills, and teahouses, becomes even more magical under the glow of lights, showcasing the quiet beauty of the season.

Winter Sparkles: Tokyo Illuminated

As the leaves fall and the city prepares for winter, Tokyo doesn't turn bleak; it lights up. The winter months in Tokyo are a spectacle of illumination, with various neighborhoods and parks decked out in thousands of LED lights, creating a festive atmosphere that warms the chilly nights.

Marunouchi: The Marunouchi area, with its stylish avenues lined with trees, becomes a tunnel of light, leading up to the Imperial Palace. The chic boutiques and cafes in the area add to the experience, making it a perfect evening outing.

Tokyo Midtown: Tokyo Midtown in Roppongi is another highlight, hosting one of the city's most dazzling winter illuminations. The Starlight Garden, a space-themed light show, is particularly popular, offering an immersive experience that feels like stepping into a galaxy of stars and planets.

Embracing Tokyo's Seasonal Shifts

Festive Foods: Each season brings its own flavors. Autumn introduces warm, comforting dishes like sweet potatoes, pumpkin, and seasonal mushrooms, while winter sees the arrival of hot pot dishes, known as "nabe," perfect for sharing on cold nights.

Cultural Festivals: Autumn and winter also host a variety of cultural and festive events, from November's Shichi-Go-San, a celebration of children's growth, to New Year's preparations and celebrations, where temples and shrines become focal points of festivities.

Winter Sports: Come winter, Tokyoites look towards nearby mountains for skiing and snowboarding. Day trips to resorts are common, offering a quick escape to winter sports enthusiasts.

Tips for Making the Most of Autumn and Winter in Tokyo

Layer Up: The temperature can vary significantly from day to night. Dressing in layers ensures comfort as you explore the city's outdoor attractions.

Stay Flexible: Weather can influence the timing of autumn leaves and the start of illumination events. Keep an eye on local forecasts and event schedules.

Off-Peak Visits: Popular spots for autumn leaves and winter illuminations can get crowded, especially on weekends. Visiting on weekdays or in the evenings can offer a more relaxed experience.

Cultural Engagement: Participate in seasonal activities, whether it's joining a tea ceremony in an autumn garden or ringing in the New Year at a temple. These experiences add depth to your visit.

During the autumn and winter seasons uncovers some cool, less-known facts and tips that can make your experience even more awesome:

Late Autumn Picnics: Even as the weather cools down, Tokyo's parks remain great spots for picnics with a view of the autumn leaves. Grab some seasonal snacks like roasted chestnuts or sweet potato treats from local vendors and enjoy the crisp air and colorful scenery.

Illumination Photo Ops: For those into photography or just looking to snap some stunning shots for the 'gram, winter illuminations in Tokyo offer unique opportunities. Try visiting illumination spots right before they officially light up for the evening to catch a less crowded view. Some places also have special photo spots set up to capture the lights perfectly.

Hot Street Foods: Tokyo's street food game stays strong in cooler months. Look out for vendors selling hot, savory snacks like takoyaki (octopus balls), yakitori (grilled chicken skewers), and amazake (a sweet, warm rice drink) during festival events. These treats are not only delicious but also perfect for keeping warm while exploring.

Hidden Onsen Spots: After a day of checking out autumn leaves or enjoying winter lights, nothing beats warming up in an onsen (hot spring). Tokyo has some hidden urban onsen spots that can give you a taste of this quintessentially Japanese experience without leaving the city.

Seasonal Shopping Deals: Late autumn and winter are great times for shopping in Tokyo, with many stores offering sales, especially around New Year (known as "fukubukuro" or lucky bag sales). It's a fun way to grab some deals on clothes, gadgets, and other goodies.

Winter Sakura: Yes, you heard that right! Certain types of cherry trees bloom in late autumn or early winter, offering a unique cherry blossom viewing experience outside the usual spring season. Places like Rikugien Garden sometimes have these winter sakura, adding a special touch to the already beautiful autumn foliage.

CHAPTER 5
PRO TIPS FOR TOKYO

5.1 CHEAP EATS

CONVEYOR BELT SUSHI AND SUPERMARKET SECRETS

Tokyo, a city famed for its culinary diversity, can surprisingly be a haven for budget-conscious foodies. Among the myriad dining options, conveyor belt sushi and the underrated supermarket finds stand out as gold mines for those looking to enjoy Tokyo's flavors without breaking the bank. This section peels back the layers on how to dine smart and savor every bite in one of the world's most exciting food capitals.

Conveyor Belt Sushi: A Whirl of Flavors on a Budget

Conveyor belt sushi, or kaiten-zushi as it's known locally, is an experience unique to Japan, blending the country's love for sushi with its penchant for efficiency and convenience. Here's why it's a must-try for anyone seeking quality sushi without the hefty price tag:

Diverse Selection: These sushi spots offer a wide range of options, from classic tuna and salmon to more adventurous choices like sea urchin and eel. Plates are color-coded by price, so you're always in control of how much you spend.

Freshness on Display: Despite the affordable prices, the sushi at these restaurants is fresh, often sourced daily from local fish markets. Watching your food come around on the conveyor belt not only adds an element of fun but also lets you see exactly what you're getting.

Custom Orders: Got a specific craving? Most conveyor belt sushi restaurants have touch-screens at each table for placing direct orders. This ensures you get exactly what you want, freshly made.

Solo-Friendly Dining: For solo travelers, these spots are ideal. There's no pressure to order more than you can eat, and the casual atmosphere makes it a comfortable choice for dining alone.

Supermarket Secrets: Discovering Tokyo's Hidden Foodie Gems

Tokyo's supermarkets are treasure troves for cheap eats, offering a glimpse into the daily culinary life of locals. Here's how to navigate these aisles for the best deals:

Ready-Made Meals: From sushi and bento boxes to fried chicken and salads, the selection of ready-made meals is vast and surprisingly affordable. These are perfect for picnics, train journeys, or a quick hotel room dinner.

Discount Hours: Many supermarkets offer discounts on ready-made food in the evening, usually starting an hour or two before closing. This is when you can grab some incredible deals, as items that can't be sold the next day are marked down.

Seasonal Specialties: Supermarkets are great places to try seasonal Japanese foods without spending a lot. Look out for seasonal fruits, limited-time sweets, and holiday-specific dishes.

Local Beverages: Beyond food, supermarkets are also great for exploring Japan's range of soft drinks, teas, and even sake. Trying different beverages can be a delightful and inexpensive way to experience Japan's drink culture.

Pro Tips for Dining on a Budget in Tokyo

Water is Free: Tap water in Japan is safe to drink, and restaurants always offer it for free. There's no need to spend on drinks if you don't want to.

No Need to Tip: Tipping is not a practice in Japan. The price you see is exactly what you pay, making it easier to manage your dining budget.

Look for Lunch Deals: Many restaurants, even the pricier ones, offer lunch sets at a fraction of their dinner prices. It's a great way to enjoy a luxurious meal without the hefty tag.

Food Courts and Basement Eateries: Department store basements and food courts often feature a wide range of eateries offering quality meals at reasonable prices. They're also a fantastic way to sample different cuisines under one roof.

Efficient Transit: Mastering Tokyo's Public Transport

Suica or Pasmo Cards: Invest in a reloadable Suica or Pasmo card for hassle-free travel on Tokyo's public transport. These cards can be used on trains, buses, and even to make purchases at convenience stores and vending machines.

Apps are Your Best Friend: Utilize apps like Google Maps or Hyperdia for real-time transit directions, train times, and platform information. They're invaluable for planning your route and minimizing transit times.

Avoid Rush Hours: Tokyo's trains are famously crowded during rush hours (7:30-9:30 AM and 5:00-7:00 PM on weekdays). Whenever possible, plan your travel outside these times for a more comfortable experience.

Smart Sightseeing: Making the Most of Tokyo's Attractions

Citywide Free Wi-Fi: Tokyo offers free Wi-Fi spots in many public areas, including train stations and cafes. Look for "Free Wi-Fi" signs or ask at information counters for access to stay connected without hefty roaming charges.

Go for Combo Tickets: Many of Tokyo's attractions offer combo tickets that provide access to multiple sites or unlimited travel on certain transport lines for a day. These can offer significant savings for intensive sightseeing days.

Early Starts: Popular attractions like the Senso-ji Temple in Asakusa or the Meiji Shrine near Harajuku are best enjoyed early in the morning, offering a serene atmosphere before the crowds arrive.

Shopping and Souvenirs: Navigating Tokyo's Retail Wonderland

Tax-Free Shopping: As a tourist, you're eligible for tax-free shopping on purchases over 5,000 yen at participating stores. Look for the "Tax-Free" sign and present your passport at the checkout.

100 Yen Shops: For affordable souvenirs and everyday items, don't miss Tokyo's 100 yen shops like Daiso and Can Do. You'll find everything from kitchenware to stationery, all at unbeatable prices.

Local Markets: For unique finds, explore local markets like Ameyoko in Ueno or the outer market of Tsukiji. These spots offer not just fresh food but also clothing, souvenirs, and local crafts.

Safety and Etiquette: Navigating Tokyo with Respect

Respect Local Customs: Tokyo is a city of unwritten rules. Remember to stand on the left on escalators, refrain from talking on your phone on trains, and dispose of trash responsibly.

Cash is King: While credit cards are increasingly accepted, many smaller shops, restaurants, and temples only accept cash. Keep some yen on hand to avoid any inconvenience.

Emergency Preparedness: Tokyo is well-equipped for emergencies, with signs and instructions in English. Familiarize yourself with basic safety tips and the location of the nearest evacuation areas, just in case.

Dive Into Tokyo's Lesser-Known Neighborhoods

Yanaka: Skip the typical tourist spots and head to Yanaka for a chill vibe. This area feels like stepping back in time, with its traditional houses and small, family-run shops. It's the perfect place for a laid-back afternoon, away from the city's frenzy.

Nakameguro: Famous for its cherry blossoms by the canal in spring, Nakameguro is a year-round hotspot for cool cafes and vintage clothing stores. The river's lined with spots perfect for hanging out and snapping some artsy pics.

Eating Out Without Emptying Your Wallet

Bento Boxes from Convenience Stores: Conbini (convenience stores) in Tokyo are a treasure trove of delicious and cheap eats. Grab a bento box, some onigiri (rice balls), or even sushi for a quick meal that won't break the bank.

University Neighborhoods for Cheap Grub: Areas around universities, like Takadanobaba or Waseda, are gold mines for affordable eats. Think ramen shops, curry houses, and cafés catering to students on a budget.

Getting Around Like a Pro

Rent a Bike: Tokyo's massive, but renting a bike can give you the freedom to explore at your own pace. Plus, it's eco-friendly and lets you discover hidden gems you'd miss by sticking to the subway.

Night Buses for Long Distances: If you're planning to travel across Japan from Tokyo, consider taking a night bus. They're way cheaper than bullet trains and you save on a night's accommodation.

Shopping Hacks That'll Save You Yen

Thrift Shopping in Shimokitazawa: For unique finds, Shimokitazawa's thrift stores are where it's at. From vintage kimonos to retro video games, you can snag some cool stuff without spending a ton.

Duty-Free Shopping: Don't forget your passport when you shop. Showing it at big stores can get you duty-free prices, which means more souvenirs or treats for yourself.

Cultural Experiences Without the Tourist Tag

Local Festivals (Matsuri): Keep an eye out for local festivals happening in neighborhood shrines. They're free to attend, super lively, and a great way to see traditional Japanese culture up close.

Join a Workshop: Whether it's a pottery class in Kichijoji or a calligraphy session in Asakusa, joining a local workshop can be a fun way to learn something new and meet people.

Staying Connected Without the Hassle

Pocket Wi-Fi Rental: Having reliable internet can save you a lot of trouble. Rent a pocket Wi-Fi at the airport for unlimited data on the go. It's perfect for navigating maps, translating signs, and staying in touch.

Safety and Etiquette: Keeping It Smooth

Quiet on the Train: Trains are surprisingly quiet places. It's cool to chat with your friends, but keep the volume down. And definitely don't chat on your phone.

Recycling Rules: Tokyo takes recycling seriously. Pay attention to the labels on bins for cans, bottles, and other waste. Keeping the city clean is a team effort.

Cash is Still King: Even in this high-tech city, cash is essential, especially in smaller shops or when heading out to more rural areas. Hit up an ATM early on so you're always prepared.

LUNCH BOXES AND CONVENIENCE STORES

Bento boxes are a microcosm of Japanese cuisine, offering balanced meals with a variety of flavors and textures in one compact package. From railway stations to local convenience stores, bento boxes are available everywhere, catering to busy commuters, students, and travelers alike.

What's in a Bento?: A typical bento includes rice or noodles, fish or meat, and a selection of pickled or cooked vegetables. The arrangement is not just about aesthetics; it's a thoughtful composition that balances taste, color, and nutrition.

Where to Find Them: Department store basements, known as depachika, are bento treasure troves, offering gourmet options that range from sushi bento to grilled salmon. Supermarkets and convenience stores like 7-Eleven, Lawson, and FamilyMart also offer a wide variety of bento boxes, with quality and freshness that might surprise you.

Why Bento?: Opting for a bento is not just economical; it's a chance to experience everyday Japanese dining culture. It's food made for the on-the-go lifestyle of Tokyoites, offering a quick, satisfying meal without compromising on taste or quality.

Convenience Stores: Tokyo's Culinary Corners

Tokyo's convenience stores, or "konbini," are legendary for their range of offerings. Far from being mere spots for emergency snack runs, these stores are integral to the city's food culture, providing a surprising array of delicious, affordable eats.

Beyond Snacks: Konbini shelves are stocked with more than just snacks. From freshly brewed coffee and bakery items to sushi rolls and onigiri (rice balls), the variety is astounding. Seasonal and regional specialties also make appearances, making each visit a new discovery.

24/7 Availability: The never-sleeping nature of Tokyo's convenience stores means you can satisfy your hunger at any hour. Whether it's an early breakfast or a late-night craving, konbini are your go-to.

Eating on a Budget: With most items priced below a few hundred yen, dining from convenience stores is a practical way to save money while exploring Tokyo. The quality of food, governed by Japan's high food safety standards, means you're getting great value for your money.

Tips for Maximizing the Konbini Experience

Try the Seasonal Specials: Konbini are known for their seasonal items, which can range from sakura-flavored treats in spring to sweet potato delicacies in autumn. These limited-time offerings are a great way to taste the season.

Heat It Up: Most convenience stores have microwaves for customers to use. Don't hesitate to ask the staff to heat up your meal for an even better dining experience.

Explore the Drink Section: The beverage selection in konbini is a world unto itself. From unique soft drinks to a wide range of teas and coffees, exploring the drink aisle is a refreshing adventure.

Make Use of the Eating Area: Some convenience stores have small seating areas or counters where you can enjoy your meal. It's a convenient option if you're looking for a place to eat your bento or onigiri right away.

Some extra layers to enhance your culinary adventure in the city, keeping it real, affordable, and absolutely delicious.

The Convenience Store (Konbini) Lowdown

Freshness Is Key: Believe it or not, konbini in Tokyo keep their food super fresh. Items like sandwiches and onigiri are restocked multiple times a day. If you're after the freshest bites, hit the store in the morning or late afternoon, right after they've restocked.

Limited-Edition Finds: Tokyo's konbini are famous for rolling out limited-edition items that often become cult favorites. Keep an eye out for these unique offerings, from seasonal drinks to anime-themed snacks. It's like a treasure hunt for foodies.

Konbini Coffee: Skip the expensive coffee shops! Konbini coffee is surprisingly good and a fraction of the price. You can get a decent cup of joe for under 150 yen, and it's perfect for those mornings when you need a quick caffeine fix.

Eco-Friendly Moves: More konbini are getting eco-conscious, asking if you need utensils or offering discounts for bringing your own cup. Participate in this movement; it's good for the planet and sometimes good for your wallet too.

Bento Box Breakdown

Department Store Delicacies: For a high-end bento experience without the high-end restaurant price, check out the basements of Tokyo's department stores (depachika). You'll find beautifully crafted bento boxes there, ideal for a fancy picnic or a special treat.

Train Station Gourmet: Ekiben (train station bento boxes) are not just convenient; they're a culinary experience. Each region's train station offers ekiben that feature local specialties. Grab one before a train journey to enjoy regional flavors on the go.

DIY Bento: Feeling adventurous? Make your own bento! Head to a local supermarket to pick up ingredients like sushi rice, seaweed, and your choice of fillings. It's a fun way to immerse yourself in Japanese food culture and customize your meal.

Extra Practical Tips

Stay Hydrated: With all the walking and exploring you'll be doing, staying hydrated is crucial. Konbini sell a wide range of beverages, from water to isotonic drinks, which are perfect for keeping your energy up.

Wi-Fi and Charging: Many convenience stores in Tokyo offer free Wi-Fi and some even have charging stations. They can be lifesavers when you're on the move and need to look up info or charge your phone.

ATM Access: Running low on cash? Konbini ATMs accept international cards, making them convenient spots to withdraw yen. Plus, they're available 24/7, so you're never left stranded without cash.

Late-Night Snacks: Tokyo's nightlife is vibrant, and whether you're leaving a club at 2 AM or finishing up at a karaoke bar, konbini will be open, ready to serve you a hot snack or a refreshing drink. It's the go-to place for night owls.

Cultural Insight: Pay attention to the seasonal changes in konbini and bento offerings; they reflect Japan's deep appreciation for the changing seasons. It's a delicious way to learn more about Japanese culture and traditions.

DINNER DEALS AND BUFFETS

Tokyo transforms as the sun sets, with neon lights flickering to life and the aromas of evening cuisine wafting through the streets. For the savvy traveler, this time of day opens up a treasure trove of dining opportunities that are both wallet-friendly and deliciously satisfying.

Discovering Dinner Deals

Early Bird Specials: Many restaurants in Tokyo offer early bird specials, tempting diners with discounted prices if they dine during the early evening hours, typically before 6 PM. It's a fantastic way to enjoy gourmet meals at a fraction of the cost.

Set Meals (Teishoku): Teishoku restaurants serve up set meals that are not only affordable but also provide a balanced plate of Japanese cuisine. A typical set might include a main dish, rice, miso soup, and pickles. These sets are filling, flavorful, and won't break the bank.

Happy Hour Hunting: Tokyo's izakayas (Japanese pubs) often have happy hour deals, serving up discounted drinks and small plates. It's an excellent way to sample a variety of Japanese dishes, from yakitori (grilled chicken skewers) to sashimi, in a lively atmosphere.

Buffet Bonanza

Hotel Buffets: While hotel dining might seem like a splurge, many of Tokyo's hotels offer dinner buffets with reasonable prices. These buffets often feature a wide range of Japanese and international dishes, making them a great option for groups with diverse tastes.

All-You-Can-Eat (Tabehoudai): Tabehoudai restaurants are a dream come true for hearty eaters. From sushi and yakiniku (grilled meat) to sweet treats like crepes and cakes, these spots allow you to indulge in as much as you like for one set price.

Vegetarian and Vegan Options: Health-conscious and plant-based eaters can also find buffet options tailored to their needs. Tokyo has seen a rise in vegetarian and vegan buffets, offering a delicious array of meat-free dishes that are kind to your wallet and the planet.

Extra Tips for Dining Smart in Tokyo

Reservations: For popular spots, especially buffets, making a reservation can save you from long waits. Some places even offer discounts for reservations made online.

Loyalty Programs: Joining loyalty programs at chain restaurants or signing up for dining apps can offer access to exclusive deals and discounts.

Local Guides: Don't hesitate to ask locals or check out community boards for recommendations. Tokyoites know where to find the best deals, and exploring based on local tips can lead to delightful dining discoveries.

Seasonal Specials: Keep an eye out for seasonal promotions, especially during holidays or festivals, when restaurants might offer special menus at attractive prices.

Late-Night Deals

Last Call Discounts: Some restaurants and even convenience stores slash prices on ready-made meals and sushi packs late at night. This is perfect for a late-night snack or a cheap meal option. Just look for the discount stickers!

Standing Sushi Bars

Sushi on the Cheap: Standing sushi bars are a game-changer for sushi lovers. They offer high-quality sushi at lower prices because they save on seating space. Plus, it's a fun, authentic experience where you can rub elbows with locals.

Explore Local Chains

Tasty and Affordable: Don't overlook local fast-food chains. Places like Yoshinoya or Sukiya serve up delicious gyudon (beef bowl) and other Japanese classics for super cheap. It's fast, tasty, and won't hurt your wallet.

University Areas

Student Deals: Areas around universities are gold mines for cheap eats. They cater to students, which means good food at low prices. Plus, you might discover some really unique cafes and eateries.

Cooking Classes

DIY Japanese Cooking: Look out for cooking classes targeted at tourists. They can be surprisingly affordable and you get to eat what you cook. It's a meal and an experience rolled into one.

Food Festivals

Seasonal Goodies: Keep an eye out for food festivals happening around the city. They often feature a wide range of eats at good prices. It's also a great way to try regional foods from all over Japan without traveling far.

Picnic Dinners

Convenience Store Feasts: Grab some goodies from a convenience store and have a picnic dinner at one of Tokyo's beautiful parks. It's super romantic and chill, plus you get to enjoy Tokyo's night views.

Share Meals

Split and Save: If you're traveling with friends, consider sharing meals. It's a great way to try a variety of dishes without ordering too much food or spending too much money.

Drink and Dine

Izakaya Hopping: Izakayas (Japanese pubs) often have great deals on drinks and small plates. Look for places with nomihoudai (all-you-can-drink) offers for the best deals.

Follow the Locals

Where the Crowds Are: A good rule of thumb is to eat where you see lots of locals. High turnover means fresh food, and local crowds often mean good, affordable prices.

Early Dinner Specials

Teishoku Spots: Keep an eye out for teishoku (set meal) restaurants that offer early dinner specials. Eating dinner slightly earlier can net you a hearty meal at lunch prices, which often include a main dish, rice, soup, and sides.

Tabelog and Other Review Sites

Leverage Local Reviews: Use Tabelog, Japan's equivalent of Yelp, to find highly rated eateries with great deals. Users often mention if a place offers unbeatable deals or set menus, giving you insider knowledge on where to dine without overspending.

Themed Nights at Izakayas

Theme Nights: Some izakayas and bars host themed nights where certain foods or drinks are discounted. Look for "Ladies' Night" deals or "Taco Tuesdays," where you can enjoy discounts on specific items.

Follow the Food Trucks

Food Truck Finds: Tokyo's growing food truck scene is a goldmine for gourmet yet affordable meals. From Mexican tacos to vegan fare, these mobile eateries offer quality food at lower prices. Check their social media for locations and times.

Combini Dinner Hacks

Upgrade Your Combini Meal: Combine various convenience store finds to create a more substantial dinner. Pair a simple onigiri (rice ball) with a side salad and some hot soup from the combini's vast selection for a balanced meal.

Soba and Udon Shops

Soba/Udon Shops: These traditional noodle shops are not only affordable but also provide a filling, quick meal. Many shops serve tempura, rice bowls, and noodles, allowing for a mix-and-match dinner under 1,000 yen.

Seasonal and Time-limited Deals

Seasonal Specials: Restaurants often offer seasonal specials or limited-time menus that provide more value. These can range from winter nabe (hot pot) promotions to summer eel dishes, aligning with Japanese culinary traditions.

Take Advantage of Lunch Sets for Dinner

Lunch for Dinner: Some restaurants package their unsold lunch sets as take-out options for dinner at a reduced price. It's a win-win: the restaurant reduces waste, and you get a quality meal for less.

Explore Residential Neighborhoods

Local Neighborhoods: Venture out to residential areas just a few train stops from major hubs. Local eateries in these neighborhoods often offer fantastic dinner deals to attract regulars.

Drink Wisely

Skip the Drinks: Opt for water instead of ordering drinks with your meal to keep costs down. If you do want to enjoy a beverage, look for places with nomihoudai (all-you-can-drink) options for a fixed price.

Buffets in Tokyo can range from traditional Japanese spreads to international cuisines, offering an all-you-can-eat format that's perfect for hungry explorers keen on tasting a bit of everything.

Scouting the Best Buffet Deals

Lunch Over Dinner: Opt for lunch buffets instead of dinner. Lunchtime prices are often significantly lower, and the spread is almost identical to what you'd find in the evening.

Hotel Buffet Promotions: Many hotels offer buffet promotions, especially during weekdays or off-peak seasons. Keep an eye on hotel websites or sign up for newsletters to catch these deals.

Coupon Websites: Websites like Groupon or local equivalents often feature buffet deals. You can find discounts for upscale restaurants and hotel buffets that would otherwise be a splurge.

Making the Most of Your Buffet Experience

Arrive Early: Getting there right when the buffet opens ensures you get the freshest food and the most choices. It's also usually less crowded, giving you a more relaxed dining experience.

Plan Your Attack: Survey the entire buffet before loading up your plate. Identify the dishes you most want to try and prioritize them. It's easy to fill up on less exciting options if you don't have a plan.

Focus on High-Value Items: To get the best bang for your buck, lean towards seafood, sashimi, and premium cuts of meat. These items are usually pricier à la carte, so indulging in them at a buffet offers great value.

Pace Yourself: It's a marathon, not a sprint. Start with smaller portions to avoid getting full too quickly. Remember, you can always go back for seconds (or thirds!).

Mind the Time Limit: Some buffets have dining time limits, usually around 90 minutes to 2 hours. Keep an eye on the clock to ensure you have enough time to enjoy without feeling rushed.

Buffet Etiquette

Don't Overload Your Plate: Take only what you can finish. It's considered bad manners to leave a lot of uneaten food on your plate, and some buffets may even charge a fee for wastage.

Wait Your Turn: Buffets can get busy, and waiting patiently for your turn, especially at popular stations, is part of good buffet etiquette.

Use the Serving Utensils Provided: For hygiene reasons, always use the serving tongs or spoons provided for each dish. Avoid using your personal chopsticks or cutlery to serve yourself.

After the Buffet

Take a Walk: After indulging in a buffet, a nice walk can be a great way to help digestion. Consider planning your buffet meal before a leisurely stroll around a nearby park or through the bustling streets of Tokyo.

Hydration is Key: With all the variety and excitement, it's easy to forget to drink water. Stay hydrated throughout your meal to aid digestion and make the most of your buffet experience.

Buffets in Tokyo offer a delightful way to sample a wide array of dishes at a fixed price, making them a fantastic option for travelers looking to indulge in Japan's culinary delights.

BEST VIEWS FOR FREE

Tokyo Metropolitan Government Building

Start your quest for free views at the Tokyo Metropolitan Government Building in Shinjuku. The twin towers of this imposing structure house observation decks that offer panoramic views of Tokyo and, on clear days, Mount Fuji. It's a popular spot for both tourists and locals, providing a bird's-eye view of the sprawling metropolis below. The decks are open until late, allowing for stunning nighttime views of Tokyo illuminated against the night sky.

Carrot Tower

Named for its distinctive color rather than any affiliation with vegetables, the Carrot Tower in Sangenjaya is a lesser-known gem for free scenic views. Located a short train ride from Shibuya, its observation deck presents an expansive look over residential Tokyo, stretching to the business districts of Shibuya and Shinjuku. It's a peaceful spot to enjoy the city's vastness without the crowds.

Odaiba's Seaside Park

For a different perspective, head to Odaiba's Seaside Park. Here, you get a waterfront view of Tokyo's skyline across the Rainbow Bridge, with the added bonus of seeing the Statue of Liberty replica. It's a favorite for photographers aiming to capture Tokyo's modernity, especially at sunset when the sky and city lights create a breathtaking backdrop.

Asakusa Culture and Tourism Center

The Asakusa Culture and Tourism Center, located opposite the iconic Kaminarimon Gate of Senso-ji Temple, offers an excellent vantage point for viewing the historic district and the Tokyo Skytree. The building's observation terrace is free to access and provides a unique angle to appreciate Asakusa's traditional atmosphere against the contrast of the Skytree's modern architecture.

Yebisu Garden Place Tower

Yebisu Garden Place Tower in Ebisu is another spot where you can enjoy spectacular views for free. The tower's observation deck gives visitors a sweeping view of Tokyo's skyline, including key landmarks and, during certain times of the year, beautiful sunsets that paint the city in warm hues.

Tips for Enjoying Tokyo's Free Views

Visit at Different Times: To fully appreciate Tokyo's dynamic landscape, visit these spots at various times of the day. Morning offers clear, sunlit views; dusk brings dramatic sunsets; and nighttime showcases the city's vibrant lights.

Avoid Crowds: While these spots are free, they can get crowded, especially during weekends and holidays. Aim for weekdays or non-peak hours for a more serene viewing experience.

Weather Check: Before heading out, check the weather. Clear, sunny days are best for distant views, especially if you're hoping to catch a glimpse of Mount Fuji.

Camera Ready: Have your camera or smartphone charged and ready. These free viewing spots offer some of the best photo ops in the city, capturing Tokyo's sprawling urban landscape and iconic features.

Combine with Other Activities: Many of these viewing spots are located within or near attractions with their own appeal. Plan your visit to include exploring the surrounding area, be it Shinjuku's vibrant streets, Odaiba's entertainment complexes, or Asakusa's historic sites.

MUSEUMS ON A BUDGET

The Tokyo Metropolitan Art Museum in Ueno Park offers a no-cost entry to its permanent exhibitions, showcasing a variety of art forms from traditional Japanese art to modern pieces. Another gem is the Sumida Hokusai Museum, dedicated to the legendary ukiyo-e artist Katsushika Hokusai, famous for "The Great Wave off Kanagawa." While special exhibitions may have a fee, the museum's permanent collection is free to explore.

Enjoy Museum Admission-Free Days

Several of Tokyo's most prestigious museums open their doors for free on specific days. The National Museum of Nature and Science, also located in Ueno Park, offers free admission on Science Day in April, providing access to its vast collection that spans from dinosaur fossils to space exploration. Similarly, the Edo-Tokyo Museum in Ryogoku, which delves into Tokyo's transformation from the Edo period to the present, has free entry days throughout the year, allowing visitors to step back in time without spending a yen.

Utilize the Grutto Pass

For those planning to visit multiple museums, the Grutto Pass is an invaluable resource.

This pass offers discounted or free entry to over 90 museums and attractions throughout Tokyo. It's an upfront investment that can save you a considerable amount over your stay, making it ideal for art lovers and history buffs eager to explore Tokyo's diverse museum landscape.

Night Museum Events

A number of museums in Tokyo participate in "Night Museum" events, where they stay open late and offer reduced admission fees in the evening. These events often include special workshops, talks, and performances, providing a unique way to experience the museum's offerings. The Mori Art Museum in Roppongi is renowned for its night-time events, offering not only stunning art exhibitions but also breathtaking night views of Tokyo from its observation deck.

Student Discounts

If you're a student visiting Tokyo, don't forget to carry your student ID. Many museums offer significant discounts for students, making it even easier to access their rich collections. The Tokyo National Museum, for example, offers a reduced admission fee for students, allowing you to wander through the largest collection of Japanese art in the world at a fraction of the cost.

Plan Around Special Exhibitions

While some of Tokyo's museum attractions may charge for special exhibitions, planning your visit around these can be particularly rewarding. These exhibitions often feature works that are not normally on display or special international collections visiting Japan. Keep an eye on museum schedules and plan accordingly—sometimes, the experience is worth the extra expense.

Cultural Exploration Beyond the Museum Walls

Remember, Tokyo itself is a living museum. Districts like Asakusa and Yanaka offer cultural experiences that rival any curated exhibition. Strolling through these neighborhoods, with their traditional architecture, temples, and artisan shops, provides a hands-on history lesson on Tokyo's evolution, cultural practices, and artistic heritage.

Diving into this cultural richness doesn't mean you have to spend a ton. Here's how to hit up Tokyo's museums without your wallet taking a hit.

Get Cultured for Free

Fire and Disaster Management Agency: This hidden gem in Yotsuya is a must-visit for the curious. It's free and you get to experience earthquake simulators, learn about fire safety, and even try on firefighter gear. It's both educational and totally Instagram-worthy.

Suginami Animation Museum: Anime buffs, this one's for you. Located in Suginami, this free museum offers a deep dive into the world of Japanese animation, with exhibits on how anime is made, plus a library of anime that you can watch.

Work Those Discounts

Museum Passports: Similar to the Grutto Pass, some museums offer their own "passport" that provides entry to multiple exhibitions over a certain period. It's a steal if you're planning a museum-heavy itinerary.

Under 18s and Students: If you're under 18 or a student, flaunt that ID. A lot of places offer hefty discounts, and sometimes free entry, making culture vulturing a lot easier on your pocket.

Time It Right

Art Night Specials: Several museums and galleries offer free entry or discounts on special "Art Nights". These events often coincide with late-night openings, so you can soak up some culture under the stars.

Anniversary Days: Keep an eye on museum anniversary dates. Some celebrate by letting visitors in for free or at a discount. It's their way of saying thanks, and your way of saying, "Score!"

Beyond the Glass Cases

Street Art Tours: Who says museums need walls? Tokyo's streets are alive with vibrant street art and graffiti. Places like Shibuya and Harajuku are outdoor galleries in their own right. Plus, it's free to explore.

Gallery Hops: Small galleries and art spaces often have free entry. Spend a day gallery hopping in areas like Roppongi or Ginza. You'll see cutting-edge contemporary art without spending a yen.

Smart Scheduling

Free Days: Many museums have a day each month with free entry. It might be crowded, but it's worth it. The Tokyo National Museum, for example, is free on May 18th (International Museum Day).

Last Admission Discounts: Some museums offer discounted tickets if you enter an hour or so before closing. It's perfect for a quick culture fix before dinner.

Tech to the Rescue

Download Museum Apps: Some museums have their own apps offering free audio guides, maps, and even discount coupons for the gift shop or café.

Social Media Stalking: Follow your favorite museums on social media. They often post about upcoming free days, special events, or temporary exhibitions.

DISCOVER TOKYO ON FOOT

Embracing Tokyo's Walkability

Tokyo is a city of contrasts, where centuries-old traditions blend seamlessly with cutting-edge modernity. By exploring on foot, you get to experience these contrasts up close, from the quiet elegance of a traditional tea house nestled in an alleyway to the futuristic buzz of Shibuya Crossing.

Themed Walking Tours

Crafting your own themed walking tours can add an exciting layer to your exploration. Consider a Historical Tokyo tour, starting in the Asakusa district with its iconic Senso-ji Temple, moving through the streets of Yanaka with its Showa-era charm, and concluding at the Imperial Palace, a green oasis surrounded by moats and stone walls.

For modern culture enthusiasts, a Pop Culture Pilgrimage could begin in the electric town of Akihabara, meander through the fashion-forward streets of Harajuku, and finish in the entertainment district of Shibuya, known for its youth culture and nightlife.

Discovering Tokyo's Green Spaces

Parks and gardens are a testament to the city's reverence for nature. A walk through the expansive Yoyogi Park, with its ginkgo tree-lined paths, or the traditional landscape gardens of Rikugien, offers a peaceful retreat from the urban rush. These green spaces not only provide a tranquil backdrop for a leisurely stroll but also play host to seasonal festivals and events that are free to attend.

Uncovering Neighborhood Gems

Neighborhoods offer their own unique vibe and hidden gems. Exploring these areas on foot allows you to discover the nuances that make each district special. The narrow lanes of Shimokitazawa are filled with vintage shops and indie theaters, while the upscale streets of Ginza showcase luxury boutiques and art galleries. Walking these neighborhoods, you stumble upon quaint cafes, local art, and street performances that capture the essence of Tokyo's diverse cultural tapestry.

Practical Tips for Urban Hikers

Comfortable Shoes: With all the walking you'll be doing, a comfortable pair of shoes is a must. Tokyo's streets are clean and well-maintained, making it easy to walk for hours.

Portable Wi-Fi or Data Plan: Having access to online maps and translation tools can be a lifesaver when navigating Tokyo's maze-like streets and communicating with locals.

Stay Hydrated: Vending machines are conveniently located throughout the city, offering everything from cold drinks to hot coffee. Carrying a reusable water bottle is also a great idea, as many parks have public drinking fountains.

Respect Local Customs: When exploring residential areas, remember to keep noise levels down and respect the privacy of locals. Tokyo is a city of close-knit communities, and mindful exploration is appreciated.

Take Breaks: Don't underestimate the size of Tokyo. Take breaks at cafes or public seating areas to rest and soak in the surroundings.

Here are more practical tips to enhance your walking tour of Tokyo:

Plan Your Route

Use Mapping Apps: Tools like Google Maps are invaluable for planning your route and estimating walking times between points of interest. They can also help you find the most scenic paths and avoid getting lost in Tokyo's complex street network.

Incorporate Rest Stops: Identify cafes, parks, or public spaces along your route where you can rest and perhaps enjoy a snack or a drink. Tokyo's convenience stores are perfect for quick refreshments.

Stay Connected

Portable Wi-Fi Rental: Consider renting a portable Wi-Fi device or purchasing a Japanese SIM card for your smartphone. This ensures you can access maps, translation services, and tourist information on the go.

Download City Guides: Offline city guides and walking tour apps can be a great resource when you're exploring Tokyo's neighborhoods. They often feature curated walks with detailed information about sights along the way.

Pack Smart

Light Backpack: Carry a small, lightweight backpack for essentials like water, a power bank, your camera, and any souvenirs you might pick up along the way.

Weather-Appropriate Gear: Check the weather forecast before heading out. Tokyo can be quite hot and humid in summer, so lightweight, breathable clothing is a must. Conversely, winters are cold, so layering is key. A compact umbrella or a raincoat is also advisable year-round due to sudden rain showers.

Cultural Considerations

Mind the Etiquette: When visiting temples, shrines, and traditional establishments, be mindful of local customs such as removing your shoes, being quiet, and not obstructing paths for photographs.

Learn Basic Phrases: Knowing simple Japanese phrases for greetings, thank you, and excuse me can go a long way in interacting with locals and navigating the city more smoothly.

Safety and Navigation

Stay Aware of Your Surroundings: While Tokyo is one of the safest cities in the world, it's still important to be mindful of your belongings and surroundings, especially in crowded areas like Shibuya Crossing or train stations.

Crosswalks and Traffic Rules: Always use designated crosswalks and follow traffic signals. Bicycles are also common in Tokyo, so watch out for bike lanes when walking.

Enjoying the Journey

Take the Road Less Traveled: Don't be afraid to veer off your planned route if something catches your eye. Some of Tokyo's best discoveries are found in its quieter, less touristy neighborhoods.

Engage with Locals: Even if there's a language barrier, a smile or a simple greeting can lead to memorable interactions. Locals can often point you to hidden gems not found in guidebooks.

Here's the inside scoop on making the most of those epic foot journeys across Tokyo, without the fluff.

Unique Spots Only Locals Know About

Hidden Cafés in Shibuya: Beyond the famous scramble crossing, Shibuya is dotted with hidden cafés that offer a peaceful retreat from the urban chaos. Look for spots above ground level – those 2nd or 3rd floor cafés often have the best views and vibes.

Yanaka – Tokyo's Time Capsule: Skip the usual and hit up Yanaka. It's one of the few places that survived the bombings of WWII, and walking its streets is like time-traveling to old Tokyo. Plus, it's cat heaven for all you feline enthusiasts out there.

Tech Hacks for the Win

Google Lens for Instant Translations: See a sign or menu in Japanese? Snap it with Google Lens for an instant translation. It's a game-changer for navigating those tricky non-English moments.

Offline Maps: Don't rely solely on Wi-Fi. Google Maps lets you download areas for offline use, so you can keep navigating even when you're off the grid.

Gear Up Right

Comfy Sneakers are Key: Tokyo involves a lot of walking. Invest in a good pair of sneakers that won't bail on you after a few miles.

Power Bank: Your phone will be your lifeline for maps, info, and translations. Keep it juiced up with a portable power bank.

Eating on the Go

Convenience Store Picnics: FamilyMart, 7-Eleven, and Lawson aren't just for snacks. You can grab a full, tasty meal for cheap and enjoy it in one of Tokyo's scenic parks or riverbanks.

Vending Machines Everywhere: Stay hydrated without paying café prices. Vending machines in Tokyo serve up cold and hot drinks at every corner, with some unique finds like hot corn soup in a can during winter.

Culture and Etiquette

Quiet on the Train: Public transport is impressively quiet. Keep your phone on silent and conversations low.

Trash Talk: Public trash cans are rare. Keep a small bag with you for trash until you find a place to dispose of it properly.

Night Walks

Odaiba at Night: For an unforgettable evening stroll, head to Odaiba. The Rainbow Bridge and Statue of Liberty replica against the night skyline are a sight to behold.

Tokyo Tower Magic: The area around Tokyo Tower at night is magical. It's less crowded, and the tower lights up the streets in a soft, orange glow that's perfect for those moody Instagram shots.

5.3 NIGHTLIFE ON A BUDGET

WHERE TO DRINK CHEAP

These establishments are more than just places to drink; they're where friends gather, colleagues unwind, and stories are shared over shared plates of delicious food and rounds of drinks.

Standing Bars: Some izakayas have no seating, and these standing bars typically offer cheaper prices. It's a great way to mingle with locals and try different small dishes without spending much.

Happy Hour Hunting: Many izakayas and bars offer happy hour specials early in the evening. Look for deals like "all-you-can-drink" for a set period or discounted prices on draft beers and house sake.

Convenience Store Hopping

Believe it or not, "conbini" (convenience stores) are a legit pregame spot in Tokyo. With a wide selection of beers, chuhai (fruit-flavored alcoholic drinks), and sake at rock-bottom prices, you can start your night here before hitting the clubs or bars.

Park Drinks: Grab your drinks from a conbini and head to a nearby park. Many Tokyoites gather in public spaces for a casual drink. Just remember to clean up after yourself.

Explore Themed Bars

Tokyo is famous for its quirky, themed bars, and some of them are surprisingly affordable. From video game bars to tiny, artist-run spaces, you can enjoy a unique atmosphere without a hefty cover charge. Just be mindful of drink prices and specials of the day.

Student Districts for Budget-Friendly Nights

Areas like Takadanobaba, Shimokitazawa, and Koenji are bustling with students and offer a plethora of budget-friendly drinking options. These neighborhoods are packed with affordable izakayas, bars, and even live music venues, where the vibe is young, energetic, and most importantly, easy on the wallet.

Nomihoudai and Tabehoudai Deals

"Nomihoudai" (all-you-can-drink) and "Tabehoudai" (all-you-can-eat) deals are a budget drinker's dream. Available in many izakayas and certain restaurants, these deals allow you to enjoy a variety of drinks (and sometimes food) for a fixed price over a set period. Always check the time limit and what's included to avoid surprises.

Tips for a Wallet-Friendly Night Out

Cash Over Card: While Tokyo is slowly embracing card payments, many bars, especially the smaller, local ones, still operate on a cash-only basis. Carrying cash not only makes transactions smoother but also helps you keep track of spending.

Skip the Snacks: It's common for bars to serve a small appetizer as soon as you sit down, known as "otoushi" or "tsukidashi." This is usually added to your bill, so if you're not hungry, it's okay to politely decline.

Local Brews Over Imports: Opt for local beers and spirits over imported drinks to save money. Japanese beers, sake, and shochu offer a taste of local flavors at a fraction of the cost of imported alcohol.

Some notable locations and districts where budget-friendly drinks are the norm, not the exception:

Shinjuku's Golden Gai

What It Is: A cramped network of six narrow alleys, lined with over 200 shanty-style bars, each with its own unique theme and character.

Why Go: Despite its growing popularity among tourists, Golden Gai retains a bohemian charm and offers surprisingly affordable drinks if you know where to look. Some bars have a small cover charge, but it's worth it for the atmosphere.

Shibuya's Nonbei Yokocho

What It Is: Also known as "Drunkard's Alley," this area near Shibuya Station is filled with tiny bars that can barely fit a handful of customers.

Why Go: It's perfect for bar-hopping and experiencing different vibes without wandering too far. Prices are reasonable, and the close-knit setting encourages friendly conversations, even with strangers.

Ebisu's Yokocho

What It Is: A lively alley packed with izakayas and bars in the fashionable neighborhood of Ebisu.

Why Go: Ebisu's Yokocho offers a more laid-back drinking experience compared to Shibuya and Shinjuku, with plenty of cheap eats to accompany your drinks.

Takadanobaba

What It Is: Known as a student district due to its proximity to several universities, Takadanobaba is home to numerous affordable eating and drinking establishments.

Why Go: The area is vibrant, youthful, and offers some of the best deals for budget-conscious drinkers. Look out for izakayas with nomihoudai (all-you-can-drink) offers.

Koenji

What It Is: A hub for indie culture, music, and thrift shopping, Koenji is also known for its affordable bars and casual dining spots.

Why Go: If you're looking to escape the mainstream and enjoy a night out without splurging, Koenji's laid-back bars and live music venues are the place to be.

Ueno's Ameyoko Market

What It Is: A bustling market by day, the area around Ameyoko in Ueno transforms at night with vendors and stalls offering cheap drinks and street food.

Why Go: It's an ideal spot for those who want to enjoy an open-air drink and soak in the lively atmosphere of a Tokyo market at night.

Sangenjaya (Sancha)

What It Is: A bit off the beaten path, Sangenjaya (often affectionately called "Sancha") is a neighborhood with a mix of old-school charm and modern chic.

Why Go: You'll find affordable drinking spots that cater to a more local crowd, offering a quieter alternative to Tokyo's more frenetic nightlife areas.

Tips for Drinking Cheap in Tokyo:

Look for Set Deals: Many bars and izakayas offer set deals that include a drink and a small appetizer. These combos are often more economical than ordering items separately.

Avoid Touristy Spots: While some popular areas have affordable options, venturing just a few streets away from tourist hotspots can lead to better deals.

Cash is King: Smaller bars may not accept credit cards, so carrying cash will ensure you don't miss out on the best deals.

Mind the Time: Some places offer discounts during off-peak hours or specific days of the week. Planning your visit accordingly can save you money.

FREE NIGHT VIEWS

Discovering the Urban Panorama

Imagine standing atop a gentle hill, the city's lights sprawling beneath you like a sea of stars grounded on earth. These moments of tranquility amidst the bustling city life are not just figments of imagination but real experiences waiting at locations where the night view is free and the memories, priceless.

Elevated Escapes

One such secret is nestled within a metropolitan government building, where access to the observatory deck transforms your evening into an aerial dance with the city. As you ascend, the day's hustle fades, replaced by a serene expanse of twinkling lights and iconic structures standing tall against the twilight sky. Here, the city tells a different story, one of quiet majesty and illuminated beauty.

Riverside Reflections

Venture towards the water, where bridges arc gracefully over rivers, their lights mirrored in the calm waters below. These riverside paths are sanctuaries for those seeking a moment of peace, with benches dotting the way, inviting you to pause and take in the view. The sight of water gently flowing, reflecting the city's lights, creates a mesmerizing tableau, blending the urban with the natural in perfect harmony.

Parks and Peaks

The city's parks, often bustling with life during the day, transform at night into vantage points for those in the know. Climbing to the top of a park's gentle rise can afford you a view unlike any other – a panoramic vista of the cityscape set against the backdrop of the night sky. Here, amidst the whisper of leaves and the distant hum of the city, you find a viewpoint that offers not just a visual feast but a moment of introspection.

Streets Alive with Stories

Walking the city's streets at night is an adventure in itself. The glow of street lamps, the buzz of night markets, and the silhouette of traditional architecture against the modern skyline create a dynamic backdrop for your nocturnal explorations. It's in these unplanned wanderings that the city reveals its hidden corners and illuminated secrets, free for all who wander with open eyes and hearts.

Navigational Nuggets

Look Up: Sometimes, the best views are above you. Rooftop gardens on buildings and malls often provide public access, offering an oasis of calm and a unique perspective on the city's night beauty.

Follow the Lights: Festivals and seasonal events often light up parts of the city in spectacular displays. Following these lights can lead you to breathtaking scenes, from illuminated temples and shrines to vibrant street decorations.

Embrace the Journey: The beauty of exploring at night is not just in the destination but in the journey. Each step offers a new angle, a different light, a fresh perspective on the city's nocturnal charm.

As you weave through the urban fabric, each step uncovers a layer of the city's nocturnal charm, revealing scenes as diverse as they are stunning, all accessible to the keen-eyed traveler.

The Observatory Haven

Perched atop one of the city's tallest buildings, a free-access observatory offers a sanctuary above the hustle. Here, the city sprawls beneath you like a living, breathing organism, its lights pulsating with the rhythm of night-time activities. The observatory, often overlooked in favor of more famous, fee-charging counterparts, stands as a testament to the beauty that can be enjoyed without a price tag. Visitors lean over the railing, whispers and gasps mingling with the soft hum of the city below, as they capture the skyline's silhouette against the velvet night.

The Riverside Chronicles

Just a stone's throw from the bustling streets, the riverbanks offer a serene counterpoint to the city's frenetic pace. Here, locals and travelers alike find respite, their silhouettes dotted along the water's edge, gazes fixed on the reflections of bridges and buildings dancing on the water's surface. The riverside, with its unhurried rhythm, invites you to slow down, to watch as boats glide silently, their lights trailing in the water, creating a spectacle of light and shadow.

The Urban Hilltop Tales

There's a hill within the city, an unassuming rise of land that, by day, offers little more than a green respite from concrete and steel. But as dusk falls and the city lights awaken, this hill transforms into a viewing spot rivaling any paid attraction. Families, couples, and solo adventurers make the trek, picnic baskets and cameras in hand, settling on the grass to watch as day turns to night and the city reveals its illuminated majesty. The laughter and music from these gatherings mingle with the distant city sounds, creating a soundtrack to a night spent under the stars.

The Story of the Wandering Explorer

The true essence of discovering the city's night views lies not in specific destinations but in the act of wandering. Each alley and street, lit by the soft glow of lanterns and neon, tells a story. From the historic district, where the past is illuminated by the gentle light of paper lanterns, to the modern avenues, ablaze with digital screens and flashing lights, the city at night is a mosaic of stories waiting to be discovered. As you walk, the cool night air brings scents of street food and whispers of conversations, guiding you through a sensory journey that costs nothing but promises rich rewards.

THE ALLURE OF THE STREETS AT NIGHT

When the sun sets, the city transforms. Streets once busy with the day's hustle turn into stages for the night's performers. Street performers, from musicians to dancers, bring corners to life with their art, offering impromptu shows that capture the essence of the city's diverse culture. Finding a spot on the sidewalk to enjoy live performances is a quintessential part of the city's nightlife, inviting passersby to stop and immerse themselves in the talent on display.

Midnight Markets: A Feast for the Senses

As night deepens, certain streets come alive in a different way, hosting midnight markets that feel like secret gatherings. Here, the air is thick with the aroma of street food, from sizzling takoyaki balls to savory yakitori skewers, each stall offering a taste of the city's culinary richness at pocket-friendly prices. Navigating through these markets, with their kaleidoscope of sights, sounds, and smells, is an adventure in itself—a feast for the senses that costs little more than the price of a snack.

Parks After Dark: Urban Oases

The city's parks, which by day serve as green refuges, don't lose their charm after dark. Instead, they become serene spots for those looking to escape the neon buzz. Groups of friends gather on park benches, sharing stories under the soft glow of street lamps, while solo wanderers find solace in the quiet, starlit paths. These green spaces offer a rare blend of tranquility and subtle urban energy, making them perfect for late-night picnics or contemplative walks, free from the constraints of time and money.

Exploring Residential Areas: Uncover Hidden Gems

Venturing into the city's residential neighborhoods reveals a different side of its night life. Away from the main tourist trails, you'll find local bars and izakayas where the drinks are cheap and the welcome is warm. These spots, often tucked away in narrow lanes, provide a glimpse into the city's soul, where the night is marked not by the clamor of crowds but by the laughter and chatter of its residents. It's here that you can enjoy the city's hospitality, savoring local drinks and snacks without the hefty price tag of more central locations.

Joining the Night Walkers

For those who prefer exploration over sitting still, joining a night walk can be an exhilarating experience. Organized groups often venture out to explore the city's landmarks under the cover of night, offering a new perspective on familiar sights. These walks, which sometimes follow themes from ghost tours to architectural explorations, are not only a great way to see the city from a different angle but also a chance to meet fellow travelers and locals, sharing in the collective experience of discovering the city's hidden stories.

Tips for Enjoying the Night on a Budget

Stay Informed: Keep an eye on local event listings and social media groups that share info on free or cheap nighttime events, from gallery openings to cultural festivals.

Travel Smart: Walking or using a bicycle can save you money on late-night taxis or rideshares, and many of the city's best night views are within walking distance of each other.

Safety First: While the city is known for its safety, always be aware of your surroundings, especially when exploring less crowded areas at night.

Here's the down-low on how to dive deep into the nightlife scene, making every moment count without spending a ton.

Dive Bars and Hidden Gems

First up, dive bars and hidden spots are your best friends for a night out on the cheap. These places have a chill vibe, friendly locals, and prices that won't make you do a double-take when you see your bill. Look for bars a couple of blocks away from the main drag—these are the places where you can grab a beer or a local drink without the tourist mark-up.

Karaoke on a Budget

Karaoke is a must-do, but renting a private room can add up. Instead, hit up karaoke places during off-peak hours, like weekday afternoons or late-night slots, when rates are way cheaper. Some places even offer all-you-can-sing deals during these times. Bonus: bringing your snacks or opting for venues that allow it can save you extra cash.

Late-Night Eats

After all that singing and exploring, you'll be starving. Skip the sit-down restaurants and head straight for street food stalls or convenience stores. You'll be surprised at how tasty and satisfying these budget-friendly bites can be. From onigiri (rice balls) to yakisoba pan (noodle-filled sandwiches), these are perfect for munching on the go.

Free Events and Festivals

Keep an eye out for free events and festivals happening around the city. From art exhibitions to street parades, these events are not only fun but also offer a glimpse into the city's culture. Plus, they're great for experiencing the city's vibe without spending a dime.

Nighttime Sightseeing

Who says sightseeing is only for daytime? Many of the city's iconic spots light up at night, offering a totally different experience compared to the daytime hustle. Walking around and taking in these illuminated sights is free and makes for awesome photo ops. Think of it as your personal night tour without the tour guide and the fees.

Public Transport Hacks

Getting around at night can get pricey, especially if you're relying on taxis. Instead, familiarize yourself with the night bus routes or consider renting a bike. Some areas are also totally walkable, which means you can soak up the vibes and sights at your own pace.

Drink Deals and Happy Hours

Scout out bars and pubs with the best drink deals and happy hours. Some places offer killer discounts or two-for-one specials, which can significantly lower the cost of your night out. Apps and local guides are gold for finding these deals, so make sure to do a quick check before heading out.

Group Fun

Everything's better with friends, including sticking to your budget. Going out in a group can sometimes snag you group discounts or special deals, especially at places looking to fill up larger tables or rooms. Plus, it's way more fun to share those late-night snacks and drinks with your crew.

Stay Safe and Smart

Finally, while you're out having the time of your life, staying safe is key. Keep an eye on your belongings, stick with your friends, and have a plan for getting back home. Remember, a night out is only as good as the memories you keep.

5.4 DODGING CROWDS

TIMING POPULAR SPOTS

The key to beating the crowds lies in the quiet hours of the morning. Iconic gardens, historic temples, and bustling markets possess a different kind of magic in the early AM. As the sun rises, these places are bathed in a soft, golden light, offering not just the perfect lighting for your photos, but also a peaceful ambiance that's hard to find any other time of the day. Imagine having a sprawling garden almost to yourself, where the only sounds are the chirping of birds and the rustle of leaves in the breeze.

Late Afternoon Adventures

While mornings are golden, late afternoons into the early evening also offer a sweet spot for exploring. Many tourists head back to their accommodations to rest or dine, leaving some of the city's busiest spots in a rare state of calm. It's during these hours that you can leisurely stroll through museum galleries, enjoy a quiet cup of tea overlooking a scenic view, or capture the perfect shot of that famous intersection without a sea of heads blocking your view.

Weekday Wandering

Timing isn't just about the hour but also the day of the week. The difference between a weekday visit and a weekend foray to the same location can be like night and day. Museums, aquariums, and attractions that see a torrent of visitors on weekends can offer a more personal experience on a Tuesday afternoon, for example. This also often means shorter lines, less waiting, and a chance to take in exhibits and sights without rush.

Seasonal Secrets

Each season brings its own crowds, with certain times of the year drawing visitors from all corners of the globe. However, there are those in-between seasons or "shoulder periods" that offer a respite from the peak tourist influx. Visiting just before or after the major holiday seasons can give you the best of both worlds: enjoyable weather and fewer people. Plus, many places have a different charm outside their busiest season—think gardens with autumn leaves rather than spring blossoms, or temples dusted with snow instead of surrounded by summer greenery.

Nighttime is the Right Time

Don't underestimate the allure of the city after dark. Not only do the crowds thin out, but many attractions light up at night, offering a completely different experience. Walking tours, night markets, and even some temples and shrines offer special evening hours, allowing you to explore these spots under the cloak of night, away from the daytime throngs.

Strategic Eating

Dining can also be an exercise in crowd dodging. Opting to eat during off-peak hours can mean getting a table at that popular restaurant without a wait. Late lunches and early dinners open up possibilities that would require reservations or long waits at other times.

Insider Tip: Local Events

Keeping an eye on local events can also guide your timing. A local festival might mean certain areas are busier than usual, but it can also mean other popular tourist spots are quieter. Similarly, knowing when local schools have their holidays can help you plan around the domestic travel peaks.

HIDDEN GEMS OVER TOURIST TRAPS

The true essence of the city often lies hidden in its narrow alleys and side streets. These are the places where you stumble upon tiny, family-run eateries that have been perfecting a single dish for generations, or quaint cafes that double as bookshops, filled with the aroma of coffee and old paper. It's in these nooks that the city's pulse beats strongest, offering a glimpse into the daily lives of its residents.

The Charm of Local Neighborhoods

Beyond the glitz and glam of tourist-heavy districts lies the charm of local neighborhoods. Here, small galleries showcase the work of emerging artists, and workshops offer a chance to dive into traditional crafts hands-on. These areas invite you to slow down and savor the city's cultural tapestry, one quiet street at a time.

Parks Off the Beaten Path

While everyone flocks to the city's famous green spaces, there are countless smaller parks and gardens that offer tranquility and beauty without the crowds. These are the spots where you can find locals practicing tai chi, reading, or simply enjoying a moment of solitude. These green havens are perfect for a picnic, a leisurely stroll, or a quiet afternoon with a book.

Nightlife Beyond the Mainstream

Forget the neon lights and the thumping music of popular nightlife spots. The city's lesser-known areas offer intimate music venues, where live bands play to a cozy room, and bars where the bartender has time to share the stories behind each drink. It's a more subdued, but deeply enriching, way to experience the city's night scene.

Seasonal Secrets Without the Crowds

Every season brings its own set of attractions, but stepping away from the seasonal hotspots reveals quieter places to enjoy the city's natural beauty. From hidden cherry blossom spots in spring to secluded autumn leaf-viewing areas, these lesser-known locations let you enjoy the season's offerings in peace.

Tips for Uncovering Hidden Gems

Ask the Locals: There's no better way to find hidden gems than to strike up a conversation with locals. They're often more than happy to share their favorite spots that guidebooks might not mention.

Explore on Foot: The best discoveries are often made when you're wandering without a destination in mind. Take different turns, venture into alleys, and see where the city takes you.

Use Social Media Wisely: Platforms like Instagram can be great for finding hidden gems. Look for geotags and local hashtags to uncover places that don't make the usual tourist lists.

The secret to a crowd-free start lies in the city's early morning calm. As dawn breaks, the streets whisper stories waiting to be heard, with historical sites and parks offering serene solitude. This is the time to enjoy the city's famed gardens and shrines, where the first light of day casts a golden hue, creating a backdrop that feels almost personal.

PLANNING YOUR DAY SMART

Crafting a Midday Retreat

As the city wakes and the crowds begin to swell, seeking refuge in lesser-known cafes or local libraries provides a peaceful respite. These midday havens are perfect for reflecting on the morning's adventures or planning your next move. Opt for lunch in tucked-away spots where the true flavor of the city can be savored away from the bustling tourist areas.

Timing Major Attractions

The key to navigating popular spots without the crowds involves timing and a bit of strategy. Late afternoons or early evenings, when many are resting before dinner, present a quieter window to explore. Additionally, targeting these attractions on weekdays rather than weekends can dramatically reduce waiting times and offer a more intimate experience.

Discovering the Night's Magic

As the sun sets, the city doesn't sleep; it simply transforms. This is your cue to venture into the illuminated night. Night markets, river walks, and illuminated landmarks offer a wholly different perspective under the cloak of darkness, with significantly fewer people. It's a time when the city's true vibrancy shines, allowing for leisurely exploration and unobstructed views.

Flexible Itineraries

While having a plan is crucial, the magic often lies in the unplanned detours. Allow yourself the flexibility to wander off your mapped route. The city is riddled with hidden alleys, boutique stores, and local art that aren't on the typical tourist radar but are often the highlights of any visit.

Utilizing Technology

Leverage apps for real-time updates on crowd sizes at major attractions, and use mapping tools not just for directions but to find interesting spots along your route. Social media can be a goldmine for discovering local events or pop-up exhibitions that offer a unique glimpse into the city's cultural scene without the crowds.

Evening Leisure

Concluding your day doesn't mean retreating to your accommodation. The city's residential neighborhoods come alive in the evening in a different, more intimate manner. Small izakayas, local eateries, and public baths offer an authentic end to your day, letting you rub shoulders with locals in settings that remain untouched by the typical tourist itinerary.

5.5 WRAPPING UP

EMBRACE THE UNEXPECTED

BRINGING TOKYO HOME

In every nook and cranny, from bustling markets to serene parks, the city hides treasures that can't be found in any guidebook. These are the moments of unexpected joy—turning a corner to find a festival in full swing, stumbling upon a tiny café that serves the best coffee you've ever tasted, or discovering a quiet spot with the perfect view of the skyline. Such serendipitous experiences remind us that sometimes, the best memories are those we never planned for.

Letting Go of Plans

While having a plan can provide direction, clinging too tightly to it can close off opportunities for genuine discovery. There's a unique kind of freedom in leaving gaps in your schedule, in deciding to explore a random subway stop or follow the sound of music down an alley. These decisions, made on a whim, can lead to some of the most enriching experiences, connecting you with the city in ways you hadn't imagined.

The Unexpected Guide

Locals and fellow travelers are often the bearers of unseen knowledge, offering recommendations that guide you to the city's hidden gems. Engaging in conversations, asking for advice, or simply observing where the locals go can redirect your journey towards paths less traveled, where the essence of the city truly shines.

Challenges as Part of the Journey

Not all unexpected turns lead to picturesque outcomes, and that's perfectly okay. Missed turns, language mix-ups, and unplanned rain might seem like setbacks, but they're also part of the adventure. These moments challenge us to adapt, to find humor and joy in the mishaps, and often lead to unexpected solutions that become memorable stories.

The Night as Your Canvas

As the day fades into night, the city doesn't wind down—it transforms. Embracing the night without a set plan invites a different kind of exploration, where illuminated streets and night markets become stages for new discoveries. Nighttime is when the city breathes differently, offering a glimpse into its soul through the vibrancy of its after-dark persona.

Embracing Local Life

The essence of any city lies in its daily rhythms, the routines of its residents, and the ordinary places that don't make it onto postcards. Spending a day living like a local—shopping at neighborhood stores, eating at a local joint, taking public transport—can open your eyes to the city's true character, beyond the tourist facade.

The Journey Within

Finally, embracing the unexpected is as much about external explorations as it is about the internal journey. Each unexpected turn, each unplanned encounter, is an opportunity for growth, pushing you out of your comfort zone and inviting you to see not just the city, but also yourself, from new perspectives.

BRINGING TOKYO HOME

In the age of instant sharing, taking a moment to capture the city through your lens with intention can create lasting mementos. Whether it's a sunrise over a serene park, the bustling energy of a street market, or the quiet elegance of a hidden café, these photographs become windows to the past, each telling a story, each evoking a feeling. Consider creating a photo journal or a digital album dedicated to these moments, a curated collection that brings the city's narrative into your everyday space.

Artifacts of Memory

Beyond the typical keepsakes, seek out items that resonate with your personal journey. A handcrafted item from a local artisan, a book from a quaint bookstore, or even a simple stone from a favorite park can serve as powerful anchors to your experience. These artifacts, rich with personal significance, serve as daily reminders of the moments of joy, discovery, and connection you found in the city.

Culinary Souvenirs

One of the most sensory ways to bring the city home is through its flavors. Collecting spices, teas, or recipes that you encountered allows you to recreate and share the culinary delights of your travels with friends and family. Hosting a dinner inspired by the meals you enjoyed not only serves as a delicious souvenir but also as an opportunity to share your journey and the city's culture through taste.

Stories and Conversations

Perhaps the most profound souvenirs are the stories you collect and the conversations they spark. Sharing tales of your adventures, the people you met, and the lessons learned along the way enriches your social circles with the city's spirit. It's in these exchanges that the essence of the city lives on, inspiring curiosity and wanderlust in others.

Creative Inspiration

Allow the city to influence your creative projects, whether it's through writing, art, music, or any form of expression that resonates with you. The city's landscapes, its people, and your experiences can fuel your creativity, leading to works that not only pay homage to your journey but also translate its impact into something uniquely personal and universally relatable.

Reflective Practices

Incorporating reflective practices into your routine, such as journaling or meditation, can help keep the city's influence alive in your daily life. Reflect on the lessons learned, the changes within, and the beauty witnessed, letting these insights guide your personal growth and perspectives.

Community Engagement

Finally, bringing the city home can mean engaging with your local community in new ways, inspired by your travels. Whether it's volunteering, participating in cultural exchanges, or simply bringing more awareness to the beauty and diversity around you, you carry the spirit of the city forward, impacting your world in meaningful ways.

SEE YOU AGAIN, TOKYO

Your time in the city leaves an indelible mark, not just in the photographs captured or the souvenirs collected, but in the way your steps have become a part of its endless story. Each visit to a temple, park, or hidden café has added layers to your understanding of the city's soul, revealing nuances and colors you hadn't noticed before. It's these experiences, these moments of connection, that beckon you to return, promising new discoveries with every visit.

The Call to Return

"See You Again" is a whisper in the bustling streets, a murmur in the quiet gardens, and a chorus in the lively markets—a call that resonates with the promise of unfinished stories and unexplored corners. The city, with its ever-changing landscape and timeless traditions, invites you to witness its evolution, to see how it grows and transforms, just as you do with each visit.

The Unexplored Awaits

No matter how many days you spend wandering its streets, the city always keeps some secrets tucked away, waiting for your return. There are always more neighborhoods to wander, more culinary delights to taste, and more cultural treasures to uncover. The anticipation of these undiscovered experiences makes the promise of "See You Again" not just a hopeful wish but a future filled with endless possibilities.

Leaving with Gratitude

Departing with a heart full of gratitude, you carry with you the kindness of strangers who became friends, the serene moments of reflection in the midst of urban chaos, and the exhilarating discovery of your own resilience and curiosity. These gifts, bestowed so generously by the city, become a part of who you are, shaping your journey long after you've left its embrace.

The Continuation of Your Story

"See You Again" is the understanding that your story with the city is not linear but cyclical.

With each return, you peel back another layer, deepen your connection, and continue the story that you and the city are writing together. It's a narrative of growth, of adventure, and of the profound joy found in exploring the world and discovering its myriad ways of being.

A Promise to Keep Exploring

As you say goodbye, you make a silent promise not just to return but to keep the spirit of exploration alive, whether you're navigating the streets of far-off cities or the familiar paths of your everyday life. The journey has taught you that exploration is not just about geography but about the willingness to see the world, and yourself, with wonder, curiosity, and an open heart.

HOW TO TREAT THIS BOOK

Consider this guide not just as a collection of destinations but as a companion on your journey. It's designed to be your gateway to experiences that resonate, whether you're navigating the sprawling urban landscape, delving into the rich tapestry of Japanese culture, or seeking moments of tranquility amidst the buzz. Let it inspire spontaneity, encourage curiosity, and foster a deeper connection with the city and its people.

What to Do Next

Armed with insights from the Tokyo Travel Guide 2024, your next steps should be about personalizing your adventure. Start marking pages, noting down must-visit spots, and perhaps even sketching out a rough itinerary. But remember, the beauty of Tokyo lies as much in its planned experiences as in the unexpected joys and discoveries that await around every corner. So, while you plan, leave room for the city to surprise you.

What to Expect

Expect Tokyo to challenge and change you. The city is a blend of the ultra-modern and the traditional, the serene and the chaotic. You'll find yourself lost in time at the Senso-ji Temple, only to be whisked back to the present by the pulse of the city's heart in Shibuya. You'll navigate through the language and the lanes, learning as much about Tokyo as about yourself. Expect to be amazed, delighted, and, at times, overwhelmed, but most of all, expect to fall in love with the city's indomitable spirit.

If Not Satisfied

We've endeavored to make the Tokyo Travel Guide 2024 as comprehensive, accurate, and engaging as possible. However, the essence of travel—and of Tokyo—is change. If there are aspects of the book that didn't meet your expectations, or if you find discrepancies, we encourage you to reach out to the publisher. Your feedback is invaluable, not just for improving future editions but also for helping fellow travelers navigate their journeys more effectively.

BONUS

Please send a mail to the mail address found it copyright section to get the automatic bonus you deserve.

JOIN OUR JOURNEY OF CONTINUOUS IMPROVEMENT

As you reach the end of this guide, we hope it has inspired and supported you throughout your travels. Our goal is to provide you with the most accurate, helpful, and engaging content possible. However, the world is always changing, and sometimes details can shift faster than the pages of a book.

If you've encountered any imperfections, outdated information, or have suggestions for how we can enhance future editions of this travel guide, we warmly invite you to share your insights with us. Your feedback is invaluable in helping us refine and improve, ensuring that future explorers have the most reliable and enriching information at their fingertips.

Please reach out to us at tokyoguide2024@gmail.com with any observations or recommendations. Whether it's a new discovery, a change in opening hours for a must-see landmark, or anything else you believe could enhance the accuracy and usefulness of our guide, we're all ears.

Your experiences and feedback not only help us grow but also enrich the travel community as a whole. We're committed to updating and perfecting our guide with your help.

Got Something to Say?

We've included a special QR code just for you. Whether you've stumbled upon a hiccup with the book, want to snag some cool bonuses, or just feel like dropping a line to the author, we've got you covered.

How It Works:

Spot the QR Code: You'll find it right here in this section. It's your golden ticket to getting in touch with us.

Scan It: Whip out your smartphone or tablet, open your camera app, and point it at the QR code. A link should pop up – tap on it!

Share Your Thoughts: Landed on the page? Awesome! Now you can report a problem, claim your bonus, or send a message to the author. We're all ears and eager to hear what you have to say.

Why We Do This:

Your feedback is like a compass that guides us in making this book even more awesome. Plus, we love connecting with our readers and making your Tokyo journey as amazing as possible.

So, don't be shy! Scan, share, and let's make your Tokyo experience something truly special.

CREDITS

Map Credits

This project utilizes map tiles designed by Stamen Design, which are made available under the Creative Commons Attribution (CC BY 4.0) license. The underlying data for these map tiles is sourced from OpenStreetMap contributors and is used in accordance with their respective licenses.

- **For Toner and Terrain Maps**:
- Map tiles by Stamen Design, under CC BY 4.0. Data by OpenStreetMap, under ODbL.
- **For Watercolor Maps**:
- Map tiles by Stamen Design, under CC BY 4.0. Data by OpenStreetMap, under CC BY-SA.

We extend our gratitude to Stamen Design for their innovative map designs and to the OpenStreetMap contributors for the invaluable data they provide. Their efforts greatly enhance the visual and informational quality of our project.

Should you wish to explore more about these maps or contribute to their ongoing development, please visit Stamen Design's website and the OpenStreetMap project page.

Foto di Nagy Arnold su Unsplash
Foto di Nichika Yoshida su Unsplash
Foto di Andrea Ferrario su Unsplash
Foto di Pablo Merchán Montes su Unsplash
Foto di Esteban Chinchilla su Unsplash

Made in the USA
Las Vegas, NV
21 June 2024